BUY NOW PAY LATER

How Debt is used to create Financial Slavery

By Paul Ifayomi Grant

Navig8or Press, Nottingham, United Kingdom
www.houseofknowledge.org.uk

Published by Navig8or Press
58 Sunnydale Road
Bakersfield
Nottingham
NG3 7GG
United Kingdom

First Printing 2009

Cover Layout by Jeremy Prince

British Library Cataloguing in Publication Data
A catalogue record for this book is available from the British Library

ISBN: 978-0954552961

Printed and bound by Tandem Press
www.tandempress.com

Dedication

This book is dedicated to:

Mwalimu Marcus Mosiah Garvey - who taught us the true meaning of mass organising

Orinthea Grant – My mother, who taught me the practice of pardner by example and who embodies commitment, sacrifice and love

Mwalimu Amos N. Wilson – who left us a 'BluePrint for Black Power'

All of the ABDF investors – who have shown vision, commitment and belief in our collective vision of economic transformation

Asante Sana for the inspiration

PAUSE FOR THOUGHT

"We have reached the time when every minute, every second must count for something done, something achieved in the cause of Africa."
Marcus Mosiah Garvey
"The Resurrection of the Negro"

"Not to know is bad, but to refuse to know is worse"
Gambian proverb

"When you know that the life and the spirit of others depend on your life and your spirit, you have no right to be afraid — even when you
are terribly afraid. In the cruel times we are living through we must find our own strength, somehow, and force ourselves to be hard."
Sembene Ousamane – *God's Bits of Wood*

Money becomes evil not when it is used to buy goods but when it is used to buy power... economic inequalities become evil when they are translated into political inequalities:
Samuel Huntington – Political Scientist

The principal power in Washington is no longer the government or the people it represents. It is the Money Power. Under the deceptive cloak of campaign contributions, access and influence, votes and amendments are bought and sold. Money establishes priorities of action, holds down federal revenues, revises federal legislation, shifts income from the middle class to the very rich. Money restrains the enforcement of laws written to protect the country from abuses of wealth—laws that mandate environmental protection, antitrust laws, laws to protect the consumer against fraud, laws that safeguard the securities markets, and many more.
Richard N. Goodwin – Speechwriter for John F. Kennedy

Big money and big business, corporations and commerce, are again the undisputed overlords of politics and government. The White House, the Congress and, increasingly, the judiciary, reflect their interests. We appear to have a government run by remote control from the U.S. Chamber of Commerce, the National Association of Manufacturers and the American Petroleum Institute. To hell with everyone else.

Bill Moyers - PBS Commentator

The abuse of buying and selling votes crept in and money began to play an important part in determining elections. Later on, this process of corruption spread to the law courts. And then to the army, and finally the Republic was subjected to the rule of emperors.

Plutarch - Historian of the Roman Republic

N.B. The photograph on the left hand side of the front cover depicting a starving Sudanese child being stalked by a vulture won Kevin Carter the 1994 Pulitzer Prize for feature photography. Shortly after taking this photograph Mr Carter committed suicide. The photograph on the right hand side of the front cover is taken from a War On Want 'drop the debt' campaign.

CONTENTS

Introduction

At the time of writing this book, the UK, US and other parts of the world were suffering the ill-effects of the 'credit crunch', caused we were told by banks and other financial institutions drastically reducing their lending to each other due to a sudden loss of confidence, precipitated by an explosion of debt, and the bursting of a speculative bubble, leading to gloomy economic performance and forecasts. This credit crunch started in the US during 2006/2007 and first hit the UK in mid to late 2007. As the saying goes; when the US sneezes Britain gets a cold and we can extend this analogy to say that when the Euro-American system gets financial influenza Afrika and Afrikans get pneumonia.

With crude oil having peaked at over $140 per barrel – before declining substantially, huge hikes in gas and electricity prices and staple food prices increasing dramatically (the price of rice doubled in a short period of time), the first half of 2008 was marked by a series of interlinked and overlapping economic crises. There were food riots in Bangladesh, Haiti, Cameroon, Egypt and many other parts of the poor world.

In the midst of all this chaos many families in the rich world faced the misery of repossessions (foreclosures) and rapidly rising unemployment and there was a growing sense of deep anxiety which always accompanies these cyclical crashes.

As usual, Afrikan communities worldwide were especially vulnerable to these systemic shock waves and our widespread economic weakness was once again brought into sharp relief.

So, this was not an especially auspicious time to bring out a product (such as a book) which taps into people's discretionary expenditure, especially as my core market, 'conscious Afrikans', tend to talk a better economic game than they fight and to be more charitable; are generally not the highest earners in the Afrikan community. In fact I had vowed in the middle of 2008 to cease book writing and publishing for at least two years as the second half of 2007 had seen a dramatic fall off in my book sales of at least 50-60%. This decline in sales had alerted me to the scale of the coming crisis.

Given the foregoing; why did I bother to write and publish this book? The short answer is; because I felt strongly that this book was needed. It is needed to give people an understanding of why Afrikan nations and so many Afrikan people have fallen into what seems like perpetual poverty. It is needed to highlight that there is nothing magical, scriptural, pre-ordained or inevitable about this situation. And most of all it is needed to give people options for changing their personal and community situation through concerted action and co-operation.

I have touched upon some of these issues in my previous books and in many ways I see all of my books as a continued exploration and re-exploration of critical issues facing Afrikan people and the world, hence the need to revisit key issues and restate key points. I will also be producing a DVD to accompany this book so there will be no excuse not to access this information. The only question will be what you choose to do with it.

Consumption and Crass Materialism in the Age of the Kali Yuga

In his wonderfully insightful book, Ancient Future (1999), Wayne Chandler provides a broader, metaphysical, framework for understanding the times we live in and contextualising those things we see around us that seem strange.

In chapter six of his work in which he explores the sixth of the seven Hermetic (Tehutian) Laws of ancient Egypt, the principle of rhythm, he cites the Mahabharata and Parenas of ancient India, books of wisdom compiled by ancient seers or prophets. In parts of these works cited by Chandler we read that:

"The barbarians will be masters of the banks of the Indus....There will be contemporary monarchs reigning over the earth, kings of churlish spirit, violent temper, and ever addicted to falsehood and wickedness.......

Property alone will confer rank; wealth [material] will be the only source of devotion; passion will be the sole bond of union between the two sexes; falsehood will be the only means of success in litigation; and women will be objects merely of sexual gratification...

He who is the strongest will reign; the people unable to bear the heavy burden, khara bara (the load of taxes) will take refuge among the valleys.... Thus in the Kali age will decay constantly proceed, until the human race approaches its annihilation...." (Chandler 1999: 180-181).

The Kali age to which the above quotation refers is one of the four yugas or ages described within the Manvantara system which describes the ""race cycles," as they apply to the evolution and deterioration of the human species under the Law of Rhythm." (Chandler 1999: 114)

Chandler goes on to tell us that "The ages or yugas are as follows:

1. Krita or Satya Yuga, which lasts 1,728,000 years, is considered the golden age, or the age of truth and purity.

2. Treta Yuga, which lasts 1,296,000 years, is also an age of purity, but less perfection than the first.

3. Dwapara Yuga, which lasts 864,000 years, is characterized by the emergence of conflicting forces and, though the cycle within this age begins in harmonious accord, it eventually exhibits the struggle between the high and low, good and evil.

4. Kali Yuga, which lasts 432,000 years, is considered by the Manvantara to be the lowest point of humanity. The human race tries desperately to rebound from the spiritual atrocities of the previous age. (The allegory of Adam and Eve being cast from the Garden of Eden.)[83]

Right now, we are in the last of these four periods, the Kali Yuga, or the "age of darkness," which is said to have begun in the year 3102 BCE with two ominous events. The first was the disappearance of the great warrior sage Krishna, the Christ of India, whose name literally means "Black One". The second event was the appearance, advance, and conquest of most of Europe and Asia by the Indo-European hordes who referred to themselves as the Hittites, Indo-Iranians, and Aryans, the latter being a name that means the "noble ones". Originating on the Eurasian Steppes circa 4000 B.C.E., the Indo-European advance became the mechanism to inaugurate the Kali Yuga....They carried with them a propensity for extreme aggression and violence as never before witnessed in our epoch." (Chandler 1999: 115-116)

Marimba Ani in her classic work 'Yurugu' (1996) also describes this Indo-European expansion around 4000 B.C.E. and Chandler in describing the culture of these merciless conquerors tells us that:

"The Indo-Europeans indoctrinated the civilisations that they subjugated with values indicative of their peculiar mind-set. These values, which have endured to the present day, embrace (1) warfare or extreme and aberrant aggression; (2) racism and segregation by color; (3) the subjugation, disdain, inferiority, and impurity of women; and (4) absence of respect and understanding of the planet and its ecosystems." (Chandler 1999: 118)

Chandler goes on to describe how these Indo-European values have become the dominant world values as Indo-Europeans conquered civilisation after civilisation and replaced matriarchal and gylany (a society where power is shared equally between men and women) based societies with a cruel and unrelenting patriarchy. The work of Chandler helps us to understand both the globalisation and entrenchment of racism and misogyny as well as how the current exploitative economics as developed by the 'Western' world has become normalised.

If one recalls the earlier quote citing the Indian prophets we should note how in the age of Kali "...wealth [material] will be the only source of devotion;" (Chandler 1999: 181). We can see the truth and manifestation of these statements in our everyday mundane lives where one can see examples of how entrenched consumerism, consumption and crass materialism have become in the age of Kali.

I was born in Edmonton, North London. Edmonton is the type of place where generally, when I am telling people where I was born, I need to make reference to another, more well known, neighbouring area, such as Tottenham, to give them a good idea as to where I am talking about. In other words; Edmonton is a pretty non-descript sort of place, however in recent years it seems to be developing a more seedy reputation for violence between young people and more bizarrely; consumer riots. Perhaps riot is a little strong; however I will leave you to judge as I describe three instances of consumer madness in Edmonton.

Poundland madness – In the late 1990's a new Poundland store opened in Edmonton Green shopping centre. Not much to write about there one would think, however one would be surprised. A friend who was out shopping on the morning of the great opening with her young daughter saw that the store was soon to be opened and joined the large crowd gathered outside. Well, as the opening time rapidly approached many in the crowd began to jostle and some started fighting. Luckily, the Police, who must have known something about the more zealous Edmonton consumers, were present to warn and in some cases arrest some shoppers in an attempt to maintain order. The situation deteriorated to such an extent that my friend was forced to ask a Police Officer to deal with a woman who was pushing and jostling so aggressively that that there was a danger that my friend's daughter would be trampled in the crush.

The Riot at Ikea – At midnight on Thursday 10th February 2005 Ikea opened a new store in Edmonton. There follows excerpts from a report in the Independent on Sunday newspaper on the chaos that surrounded the store opening.

Battle of Edmonton: chaos as 6,000 rush for bargains at Ikea opening

By Terry Kirby, Chief Reporter
Friday, 11 February 2005

"For 12 hours, Karyn Christian was among those who waited patiently at the head of the queue outside Ikea's new store in north London on Wednesday, ready to snap up the amazing offers when the doors opened at midnight.

With prices as low as £45 for a three-seater leather sofa and £30 for a double-bed frame, the bargains seemed too good to miss. Unfortunately, some 6,000 other people felt the same way.

When midnight arrived, the crowd stormed the doors and pandemonium reigned among those who managed to get inside, with tempers flaring, threats being exchanged and punches being thrown. The store had to close after unprecedented scenes which left 20 people being treated for heat exhaustion and about half a dozen needing treatment in hospital for minor injuries.

Ms Christian, 38, a civil servant, said: "There were people who each had one end of a sofa and were pulling in different directions, both shouting, 'It's mine.' Some were lying on sofas that people were trying to take away. It was total chaos. In fact, chaos was an understatement. I've never seen anything like it in my life."

As the seventh person in the queue, Ms Christian had been given a voucher and assured of being among the lucky 500 to get a sofa. But she sprained an ankle in the crush and had to scrap the rest of her planned purchases and abandon her car.

Yesterday, the doors remained firmly shut, with security guards turning away a stream of potential customers, some of whom had travelled from many parts of the South-east. Meanwhile managers of Ikea in Britain and Sweden conducted an agonised post-mortem into what went horribly wrong on Wednesday night. The store is expected to quietly reopen today or tomorrow, with its opening offers rescinded.

"We are really, really sorry. We are in total shock," said John Olie, Ikea's deputy country manager for the UK. He admitted that Ikea had not been prepared for 6,000 people to turn up and that its 700 employees and 45 security guards had been overwhelmed. "I've been involved with all our other 12 store openings in the United Kingdom, when we have had similar offers, and we have only ever had about 2,000 people turning up," Mr Olie said.

At 28,500 sqft, the store, just off the North Circular Road in Edmonton, is the largest Ikea branch in Britain,.... Advertisements featuring the bargains, urging people to come before 3am to snap one up, had been placed this week in local newspapers and Tube stations.

David Lammy, Labour MP for Tottenham, said: "Ikea must have

known that opening the store next to the second most deprived constituency in London people would flock to their store in large numbers. They did not put in place the right infrastructure to deal with that."

He was backed by one potential customer yesterday. "This is a classy place, for Tottenham. Who wouldn't want a £45 settee around here?" said Bee McKenzie, 31.........

As midnight approached, the crowds began to grow. The Ikea car park failed to cope, traffic backed up on to the dual carriageway of the North Circular, one of London's busiest roads, jams built up and some drivers panicked at not being able to reach the store. "It was dog eat dog up on the roundabout," said Carole Forster, 56, from Norfolk. Cars drove across roundabouts and reversed up the dual carriageway into oncoming traffic. Others parked illegally on the side of the road or on pavements.

Merrison Gittens, 48, from Luton, said ..... customers had repeatedly warned security guards that the crowds were likely to storm the store. "A lot of the security men just ran away."

Inside, Mr Olie said it had all been going "very smoothly" as the first people were let in. "But then they gathered all around the store and tried to come in through all the doors. We closed the doors and tried to let in one person at a time but then they came in force."

Emma Wilson, 18, from Essex, said the crowd "charged towards the entrance". She said: "Both my dad and boyfriend who had been queuing with me were taken out of sight and I was crushed against the concrete pillar and into the rows of shopping trolleys. I stood screaming because I was so scared."

Police reinforcements arrived to keep order, but upstairs conflict broke out amid the furniture and at least one child had to be lifted to safety above people's heads. Ikea managers, fearing a Hillsborough-style disaster, decided to close the store. It had been open just 42 minutes.

Mr Olie said Ikea would be reviewing its policy on openings. However, there are precedents - in September, three people died and 16 were injured in a crush when Ikea opened a store in Jeddah, Saudi Arabia."

Insanity at ASDA – In September 2008 a new ASDA superstore opened in Edmonton Green shopping centre on the site of the old leisure centre where I had spent many a happy hour during my youth. On the appointed day the store was due to open at 10.00am and I was amazed to find out that some shoppers started queuing at 4.00am to get hold of some pretty unspectacular special offers. As in the previous cases, by opening time there was a seething mass of hungry consumers salivating at the entrance and discord, threats and violence naturally ensued.

So what can one learn from the fact that in an inconspicuous area of London, people; for the most part on low to medium incomes, will jostle, swear and in some cases fight to be first in line at the opening of a new Ikea, ASDA or pound shop! In my view it highlights on a very everyday mundane level the metaphysical truths described earlier by the seers of ancient India. We live in an age of low consciousness, of spiritual debasement where the external and material are valorised and the internal and spiritual given scant attention. Because when compared to the cycles of human history let alone the cycles of the Earth's history (4.5 billion years), an individual lifetime is so short that we come to believe that what we are experiencing is 'normal'. If normality can be defined as "life giving or life affirming behaviour" (Nobles) then we live in highly abnormal times, even though predicted as inevitable by the ancient sages.

All that to say this. Whilst we have to deal with the temporal, everyday, material aspects of life (which are the subject for discussion of this book) we should never lose sight of the fact that there is a higher, deeper meaning to our existence, the understanding of which humanity has spent much of its existence seeking and that meaning is not to be first in the queue outside of Poundland!

SECTION I

The Poverty Makers, Economic Rapists at Work

ENSLAVEMENT AND THE HISTORICAL BASIS FOR AFRIKAN IMPOVERISHMENT

DESCRIPTION OF A SLAVE SHIP

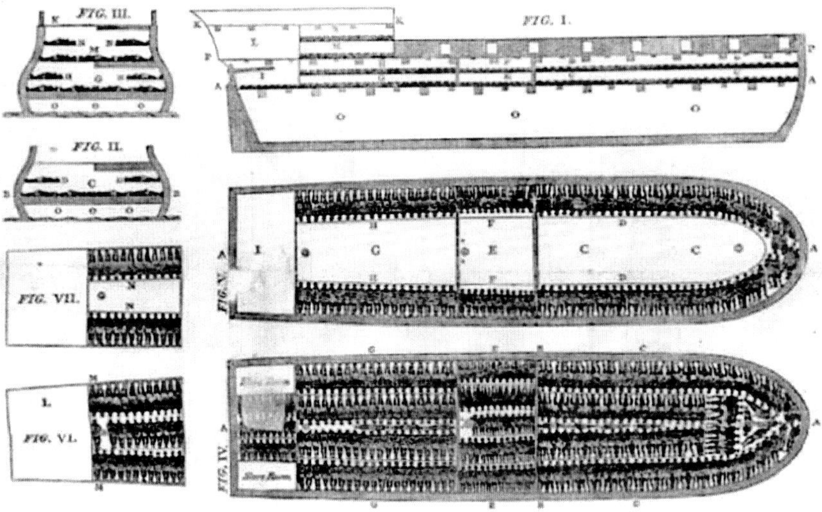

www.pbs.org/wgbh/aia/part1/1h295b.html

In his groundbreaking book, 'How Europe Underdeveloped Africa', Walter Rodney in looking at the question of the population effects of the kidnapping and enslavement of Afrikans during the European trade in enslaved Afrikans, tells us:

"No one has been able to come up with a figure representing total losses to the African population sustained through the extraction of slave labour from all areas to all destinations over the many centuries that slave trade existed. However on every other continent from the fifteenth century onwards, the population showed constant and sometimes spectacular natural increase; while it is striking that the same did not apply to Africa. One European scholar gave the

following estimates of world population (in millions) according to continents:

	Year			
Continent	**1650**	**1750**	**1850**	**1900**
Africa	100	100	100	120
Europe	103	144	274	423
Asia	257	437	656	857

None of the above figures is really precise, but they do indicate a consensus amongst researchers on population that the huge African continent has an abnormal record of stagnation in this respect, and there is no causative factor other than the trade in slaves to which attention can be drawn.

An emphasis on population loss as such is highly relevant to the question of socio-economic development. Population growth played a major role in European development in providing labor, markets, and the pressures which led to further advance. Japanese population growth had similar positive effects; and in other parts of Asia which remained pre-capitalist, the size of the population led to a much more intensive exploitation of the land than has ever been the case in what is still a sparsely peopled African continent.

So long as population density was low, then human beings viewed as units of labor were far more important than other factors of production such as land." (Rodney 1981: 97-98)

Rodney notes how European scholars have a marked tendency to concentrate on the numbers of Afrikans "landed alive in the Americas, the Atlantic Islands, and Europe." (Rodney 1981: 96) The estimates by these European scholars of the numbers of Afrikans landed in these geographical regions has tended to coalesce around the 10-12 million figure. However these estimates do not include or take account of the following factors in terms of the actual numerical impact of enslavement:

1. The loss of life during the 'Middle Passage' (between 15-25% depending upon period)

2. The loss of life in the slave dungeons
3. The loss of life during the long treks (often hundreds of miles) to the dungeons
4. The loss of life during the capture of Afrikans
5. The wars and conflicts generated as a result of the enslavement trade (Rodney indicates that warfare was the primary means of obtaining captives)

Some of the other effects of the enslavement process which Rodney suggests had a deleterious effect upon economic development in Africa include:

- Loss of population leading to the abandonment of certain environments (for example where the tsetse fly was present. Rodney suggests that harnessing nature is a fundamental part of the development process.
- Enslavement led to increases in social violence which created instability and insecurity which are incompatible with economic development
- Rodney describes how the enslavement trade was central in undermining the "Gold coast economy and destroying the gold trade." (Rodney 1981: 99)
- The energies of the most developed states in West Afrika were diverted from self-improvement and betterment to dealing with the impact of enslavement.
- Overall, the enslavement trade had a negative overall impact on agricultural production. As an example he cites Dahomey (roughly present day Benin) which "in the sixteenth century was known for exporting food to parts of what is now Togo, was suffering from famines in the nineteenth century." (Rodney 1981: 99)
- Enslavement affected areas of Africa not directly involved (either in raiding or being raided for captives) in the process since it inhibited trade and positive interaction between these areas and those implicated in the trade.
- The enslavement trade led to technological stagnation in

Afrika. The 'technology gap' between Europe and West Afrika - for example in cloth manufacture – in the fifteenth century was relatively small, however by the commencement of the colonial period during the nineteenth century the gap had increased markedly and Africa was "concentrating almost entirely on the export of raw cotton and the import of manufactured cotton cloth." (Rodney 1981: 104)

- The trade removed millions of youth and young adults (aged 15-35) "who are the human agents from whom inventiveness springs." (Rodney 1981: 105)

Rodney nails the oft quoted myth that Britain and other European powers intervened in Afrika in the nineteenth century to prevent continued enslavement. He tells us that "Britain took self-righteous delight in putting an end to Arab slave trading, and in deposing rulers on the grounds that they were slave traders. However in those very years, the British were crushing political leaders in Nigeria, like Jaja and Nana, who had by then ceased the export of slaves, and were concentrating instead on products like palm oil and rubber........The common factor underlying the overthrow of African rulers in East, West, Central, North and South Africa was that they stood in the way of Europe's imperial needs." (Rodney 1981: 138)

The Arab Enslavement of Afrikans

We do not have space within the confines of this book to examine in detail this important aspect of the Maafa (Ani: 1996) which so damaged Afrikan people. Namely the kidnapping, enslavement and torture of Afrikans by Arabs which commenced well over one thousand years ago and continues to this day in places such as Mauritania and Sudan (in the latter case involving a genocidal campaign mainly perpetrated by Arabised Afrikans or cultural Arabs i.e. Black people who have a psychopathic hatred of their own Blackness which they project onto other Black people [including Black Muslims] who are comfortable with being Black). There are a series of articles by the Nigerian scholar Dr Chinweizu which can be found on my website *www.houseofknowledge.org.uk* in which he seeks to promote what he refers to as Black Power Pan Africanism as opposed to the Continentalist version of Pan-Africanism, most famously promoted by Kwame Nkrumah and which was first put into the public domain as an ideological position by others in around 1945. In these essays Dr Chinweizu exposes Arab colonialism and racist ideology and compares it to that practiced and espoused by Europeans. If you go to the website you will find that the similarities are striking.

In his essay 'COMPARATIVE DIGESTS 1] Racism: Arab and European compared' (2007) Chinweizu examines how racism is manifested within these two conquering groups under the following headings: Doctrines, Stereotypes, One drop rule, Social strata; Economic and legal inequality, Sexual stereotypes, Stereotypes in literature, Ideological/Theological legitimation, Colorism: discrimination on basis of skin color, and Opportunity Limited by color: Blackness as an Affliction.

There follows some excerpts from this essay to give the reader a flavour of how Arab racism towards Afrikans has been expressed in strikingly similar terms to that of Europeans.

Doctrines

A Persian treatise on world geography, written in 982 AD says:

"As regards southern countries, all their inhabitants are black on account of the heat of their climate. Most of them go naked. . . . They are people distant from the standards of humanity." And of the Zanj: "Their nature is that of wild animals. They are extremely black."

See Lewis, Race and Color in Islam, pp. 35

The great geographer, Idrisi (1110-1165), ascribes "lack of knowledge and defective minds" to the black peoples. Their ignorance, he says, is notorious; Men of learning and distinction are almost unknown among them.

See Lewis, Race and Color in Islam, pp.37

Even such luminaries as Ibn Sina [Avicenna (980-1037), the most famous and influential of the philosopher-scientists of Islam], considered blacks to be "people who are by their very nature slaves."
"Blasphemy Before God: The Darkness of Racism In Muslim Culture" by Adam Misbah al-Haqq

Sa 'id al-Andalusi (1029-1070) a qadi of Toledo:
"They lack self-control and steadiness of mind and are overcome by fickleness, foolishness and ignorance, Such are the blacks, who live at the extremity of the land of Ethiopia, the Nubians, the Zanj and the like..." ... The 13th century Persian writer Nasir al-Din Tusi remarks that the Zanj differ from animals only in that "their two hands are lifted above the ground," and continues "Many have observed that the ape is more teachable and more intelligent than the Zanj." *See Lewis, Race and Color in Islam, pp.35, 36, 38*
(Chinweizu 2007:1)

Sexual Stereotypes

Immense potency and unbridled sexuality was ascribed to the black male; and incandescent sexuality was ascribed to the black woman e.g. in the poem "How many a tender daughter of the Zanj walks about with a hotly burning oven as broad as a drinking bowl"
– Farazdaq, *See Lewis, Race and Slavery in the Middle East, p.94*
(Chinweizu 2007:3)

Ideological/Theological legitimation

The Curse of Ham

Classic Muslim thought maintained that blacks became legitimate slaves by virtue of the color of their skin. The justification of the early Muslim equation of blackness with servitude was found in the Genesis story so popularly called "the curse of Ham," in reference to one of Noah's sons... In the Arab-Muslim version, blacks are cursed to be slaves and menials, Arabs are blessed to be prophets and nobles, while Turks and Slavs are destined to be kings and tyrants...

The famous Al-Tabari, for example, cites no less than six Prophetic traditions which seek to support this story. One tradition reads:

Ham begat all those who are black and curly-haired, while Japheth begat those who are full faced with small eyes, and Shem begat everyone who is handsome of face (Arabs of course) with beautiful hair. Noah prayed that the hair of Ham's descendants would not grow past their ears, and wherever his descendants met the children of Shem, the latter would enslave them...

[egalitarian] reports [were overshadowed by] the more deeply rooted tradition of racial bigotry . . . [emphasized by] Muslim geographers and travelers who ventured into Africa. . . . . Al-

Maqdisi [tenth century] wrote, " . . . As for the Zanji, they are people of black color, flat noses, kinky hair, and little understanding or intelligence." ... Ibn Khaldun (d. 1406CE) added that blacks are "only humans who are closer to dumb animals than to rational beings." ... Even such luminaries as Ibn Sina considered blacks to be "people who are by their very nature slaves." ...

The creation or resurgence of the mythology of Ham also made dark-skinned people synonymous with servitude in lightskinned Muslim thinking. This went so far that eventually the term abd (slave) went through a semantic development and came to specifically refer to "black slave" while light-skinned slaves were referred to as mamluks. And further on in later usage, the Arabic word abd came to mean "black man" of whatever status ...

– from "Blasphemy Before God: The Darkness of Racism In Muslim Culture" by Adam Misbah al-Haqq, MuslimWakeup.Com

http://www.muslimwakeup.com/archives/000498.php

(Chinweizu 2007:5)

Colorism: discrimination on basis of skin color

[In Arab culture, there is] the emotional content attached to the concepts of blackness and whiteness—the idea that black is connected with sin, evil, deviltry and damnation, while white has the opposite associations. *See Lewis , Race and Slavery in the Middle East, p.94*

Colorism in Sudan

Arab culture standardizes the white color, and despises the black color. . ..They say al-husnu ahmar (beauty is white)... [In Northern Sudanese culture] the first color in ranking is asfar. This literally means "yellow", but used interchangeably with ahmar to denote "whiteness"... ahmar (white) is the ultimate standard color for the average Northerner. It is considered the standard color of the in-group, i.e. the center of the Arab identity... The second in ranking is asmar. This literally means reddish, but it is used to describe a range of color shades from light to dark brown. This range usually includes subdivisions such as dahabi (golden), gamhi (the color of ripe wheat), and khamri (the color of red wine). The third in ranking is akhdar. This literally means green, but it is used as a polite alternative of the word "black" in describing the color of a dark Northerner... The early Arabs used the word akhdar to describe people of unquestionable nobility whose color, for one reason or the other, was black... Last and least is azrag. This literally means "blue", but it is used interchangeably with aswad to mean "black", which is the color of the 'abid... Janice Boddy shows how the women of Hofriyat village are conscious of skin color. To them, "white skin is clean, beautiful, and a mark of potential holiness". They repeatedly told her that, as a white woman, she had far greater chances to get into heaven, if she converted to Islam, than them or any other Sudanese. Their reasoning was that "this is because the Prophet Mohammad was white, and all white-skinned peoples are in the favored position of belonging to his tribal group." ... Northerners showed readiness to intermarry with white people, be they Europeans or Arabs, but they demonstrated reluctance to intermarry with black people, be they Southerners or Africans in general... Northerners usually experience [a feeling of dismay] when they discover, for the first time, that they are considered blacks in Europe and America. It is also observed in their attitude towards the black communities there... Northerners attitude towards the black population in these countries [Europe and America] is similar to their attitude towards the [Sudanese] Southerners. They usually refer to them by the word "abid' [slave], and one of my interviewees, once, referred to the Afro Caribbeans as

Southerners 'janubiyyin
Al-Baqir al-Afif Mukhtar "Crisis of Identity in Northern Sudan" (Chinweizu 2007: 6)

Hopefully the foregoing has provided sufficient evidence to demonstrate that the Arab enslavement of Afrikans was underpinned and justified by the same type of virulent racism as gave momentum to the European enslavement of Afrikans, and together they form a sustained genocidal assault unparalleled in its longevity and impact. Afrikan Muslims seem to have a harder time acknowledging and confronting Arab Muslim racism than Afrikan Christians have in accepting European Christian racism, however accept it they must if Afrikan people – irrespective of religion - are to get out from under the heel of both Europeans and Arabs.

In terms of explaining why there are not the same types of numbers of Afrikans in Arabia as one finds in the United States, Brazil and the Caribbean Chinweizu cites Lewis, who tells us that:

"An obvious question, since so many blacks entered the central lands over so long a period, is why they have left so little trace? There is nothing in the Arab, Persian and Turkish lands that resembles the great black and mulatto populations of North and South America. One reason is obviously the high proportion of eunuchs among black males entering the Islamic lands. Another is the high death rate and low birth rate among black slaves in North Africa and the Middle East. In about 1810, Louis Frank observed in Tunisia that most black children died in infancy, and that infinitesimally few reached the age of manhood. A British observer, some thirty years later, found conditions even worse:

"The mortality among the slaves in Egypt is frightful,—when the epidemical plague visits the country, they are swept away in immense multitudes, and they are the earliest victims of almost every other domineering disease. I have heard it estimated that five or six years are sufficient to carry off a generation of slaves, at the end of which time the whole has to be replenished."

Lewis, Bernard (1990) Race and Slavery in the Middle East, New York: Oxford University Press p 84 cited in 'Black Enslavement:

Arab and European Enslavement Compared, Black Power Pan Africanism' (BPPA) TRACT#2 © Chinweizu 2007

"When considering this Maafa (Ani 1996) Kiarri T-H Cheatwood tells us that "..not only must Afrikan chattel slavery be understood as unprecedented human horror, it must be understood, too as an unprecedented, self-generating ...and, to date, endless pogrom which as a process, has extended over the course of in excess of 2.5 millennia." (Cheatwood 1995:35) Cheatwood's reference to 2500 years encompasses the broader Eurasian/Indo-European assault on the Afrikan continent. In this book he identifies the Hyksos assault on Kemet between 1720 and 1675 BCE as "the first major Caucasian devastation" (Cheatwood 1995 :30) whilst earlier in this work I refer to the Indo-European expansion commencing around 4000BCE. Whichever point in time one chooses the critical lessons cited above remain the same.

FAST FORWARD TO 2009

In an article on the Inter Press Service (IPS) website entitled: Africa May Face 'Centuries' of Poverty, David Cronin in summarising the findings of a report by Social Watch reports that **"Extreme poverty will continue to blight sub-Saharan Africa for another 200 years unless action to overcome it is intensified, a new report has suggested.**

Social Watch, a network of campaigning groups, has devised a measure known as the "basic capabilities index" to assess the level of hardship throughout the world.

Its latest report finds that 80 countries – home to half the world's population – fare badly when three criteria are examined: the number of children who die before their fifth birthday, the proportion of children who complete primary education, and the proportion of births that are attended by trained midwives or other medical professionals.

Only 16 of these countries have registered considerable improvement since 2000. Although the countries making progress include India, home to 1.6 billion, regression has been recorded in others with a combined population of 150 million. The latter category includes Chad, Niger, Malawi, Benin and Yemen, while

Bangladesh, Uganda, Nigeria, Madagascar and Ghana have been listed as stagnant.

While much of sub-Saharan Africa has recorded strong economic growth in recent years, this has not translated into a major drop in poverty levels. As things stand, the basic needs of millions of Africans will not be met until the 23rd century, with many governments struggling to fulfil pledges they have made. Zambia, for example, has undertaken to provide free basic health care for all citizens, yet continues to have one of the lowest rates of life expectancy on the planet."

Cronin goes on to comment on how the many anti-poverty campaigners have been complaining vociferously about the skewed nature of aid programmes emanating from the European Union. He tells us that "Simon Stocker from Eurostep, an alliance of anti-poverty groups, said that the EU's development aid activities pay greater heed to investment opportunities for western firms in poor countries than to health and education needs. Of 70 aid plans drawn up by EU officials for Africa, the Caribbean and the Pacific, health and education have been identified as priorities in less than 10 cases each.

"Partly because the European Union is itself built around an economically liberalised approach to development, this is automatically being exported (in its aid activities)," he said. "It looks more as if the European Union is promoting its own trade interests rather than the economic development of (aid recipient) countries themselves." (Cronin 08 Jan 2009)

http://ipsnews.net/news.asp?idnews=45335

The extracts from the article by David Cronin should disabuse those of us who are naive enough to believe that 'things can only get better' for Afrika or Afrikan people. Real economic development is not inevitable; it has to be created in the face of hostile wolves masquerading as sheep who seek to perpetuate the economic rape of the continent and its people. Chattel slavery may have come to an end for most Afrikans (not forgetting its systematic continuation in Mauritania) however it has been replaced by economic serfdom and an unrelenting grinding poverty for most on the continent. The following article from the Financial Times newspaper website *www.ft.com* starkly illustrates the growing economic recolonisation of Africa through land acquisition.

US investor buys Sudanese warlord's land

By Javier Blas and William Wallis
Published: January 9 2009 23:18

"A US businessman backed by former CIA and state department officials says he has secured a vast tract of fertile land in south Sudan from the family of a notorious warlord, in post-colonial Africa's biggest private land deal.

Philippe Heilberg, a former Wall Street banker and chairman of New York-based Jarch Capital, told the Financial Times he had gained leasehold rights to 400,000 hectares of land – an area the size of Dubai – by taking a majority stake in a company controlled by the son of Paulino Matip.

Mr Matip fought on both sides in Sudan's lengthy civil war but became deputy commander of the army in the autonomous southern region after a 2005 peace agreement.

The deal, between Mr Heilberg's affiliate company in the Virgin Islands and Gabriel Matip, is a striking example of how the recent spike in global commodity food prices has encouraged foreign investors and governments to scramble for control of arable land in Africa, even in its remotest parts.

In contrast to land deals between foreign investors and governments, Mr Heilberg is gambling on a warlord's continuing control of a region where his militia operated in the civil war between Khartoum and south Sudan.

"You have to go to the guns, this is Africa," Mr Heilberg said by phone from New York. He refused to disclose how much he had paid for the lease.

Jarch Management Group is linked to Jarch Capital, a US investment company that counts on its board former US state department and intelligence officials, including Joseph Wilson, a former ambassador and expert on Africa, who acts as vice-chairman; and Gwyneth Todd, who was an adviser on Middle Eastern and North African affairs at the Pentagon and under former president Bill Clinton at the White House.

Laws on land ownership in south Sudan remain vague, and have yet to be clarified in a planned land act. For this reason, some foreign experts on Sudan as well as officials in the regional government, speaking on condition of anonymity, doubted Mr Heilberg could assert legal rights over such a vast tract of land. The deal is second only in size to the recent lease of 1.3m hectares by South Korea's Daewoo from the government of Madagascar.

Mr Heilberg is unconcerned. He believes that several African states, Sudan included, but possibly also Nigeria, Ethiopia and Somalia, are likely to break apart in the next few years, and that the political and legal risks he is taking will be amply rewarded.

"If you bet right on the shifting of sovereignty then you are on the ground floor. I am constantly looking at the map and looking if there is any value," he said, adding that he was also in contact with rebels in Sudan's western region of Darfur, dissidents in Ethiopia and the government of the breakaway state of Somaliland, among others.

The company was embroiled in a dispute with the south Sudan government over its claims to exploration rights for oil.

Mr Heilberg said Jarch had no expertise in agricultural development but would be seeking joint venture partners to cultivate the land, which is in one of the remotest parts of Sudan, in a region bordering the Nile river but with no tarred roads." (Blas and Wallis 2009)

So there you have it. The most distasteful ménage a trois possible between global capital, former US government officials/advisors and corrupt, brutal governments in Afrika. The land is literally being sold out from beneath the people's feet and this article clearly highlights the reality that there are powerful foreign investors who have a vested interest in promoting instability and the break up of nation states in Afrika. When one considers the role of the US government in Somalia one should be under no illusions that these predatory corporations not only work with the approval of the US government, but in many cases at its behest.

The photo below which accompanied the above FT (Financial Times) article depicts the area in Sudan discussed in the article as well as highlighting other Afrikan land grab deals involving foreign corporations.

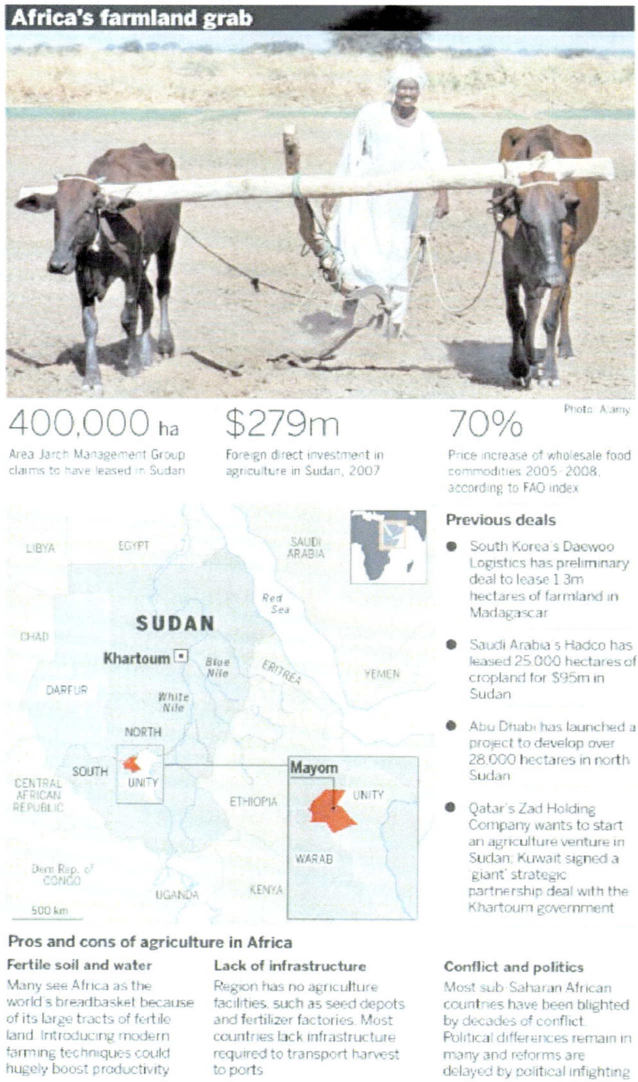

http://www.ft.com/cms/s/0/a4cbe81e-de84-11dd-9464-000077b07658.html?nclick_check=1

Bankers - Predators in Pinstripe Suits

"Historically, the United States has been a hard money country. Only [since 1913] has the United States operated on a fiat money system. During this period, paper money has depreciated over 87%. During the preceding 140 year period, the hard currency of the United States had actually maintained its value. Wholesale prices in 1913... were the same as in 1787." — **Kenneth Gerbino** former chairman of the American Economic Council

"Some people think the Federal Reserve Banks are US government institutions. They are not... they are private credit monopolies which prey upon the people of the US for the benefit of themselves and their foreign and domestic swindlers, and rich and predatory money lenders. The sack of the United States by the Fed is the greatest crime in history. Every effort has been made by the Fed to conceal its powers, but the truth is the Fed has usurped the government. It controls everything here and it controls all our foreign relations. It makes and breaks governments at will." — **Louis McFadden** (1876-1936) US Congressman (R-PA) (1915-1935), Chairman of House Banking and Currency Committee. Poisoned in 1936. Date: June 10, 1932

The information contained in this chapter has been largely gleaned from the excellent documentary entitled 'Money as Debt' by Paul Grignon and produced by Moonfire Studio (a Lifeboat News Video Production) which can be viewed on YouTube or *www.moneyasdebt.net*.

What is money?

Money is quite simply any intermediary substance or material that is used to facilitate the exchange of goods and services.

Over the course of human history a wide variety of items have been used as what we now call money. These have included cocoa beans, feathers, cowrie shells etc. As long as the item was transportable and widely accepted in a particular community it could be used as money. Over time gold and silver became increasingly popular due to their ease of transportation, physical resilience, attractiveness of appearance and relatively restricted supply.

As a result Goldsmiths became increasingly important and they had the role of casting coins whose weight and purity was certified. As their stocks of gold increased they eventually created vaults to store their precious commodity. The creation of these vaults soon led to a demand to rent space from depositors. The goldsmiths provided depositors with claim cheques as receipts for their deposits.

Soon the goldsmiths realised that their cheques were being traded in the marketplace and that depositors rarely actual removed their deposits. Paper money was also more convenient than heavy gold coins.

The goldsmiths also lent out their gold and charged interest. Borrowers eventually began to ask for claim cheques rather than gold. After a while the goldsmiths began to lend against depositors' gold as well as their own and earned interest on this new lending as well.

The birth of banking and invisible money

Goldsmiths became very rich and eventually depositors began to demand a slice of the pie, by way of interest payments on their deposits and this was how modern banking was born.

At this stage the bankers came up with an ingenious idea to make more money. They began to lend against gold that did not exist i.e. their lending exceeded their deposits. As lending grew and grew people became increasingly suspicious and borrowers began to demand gold instead of paper cheques. Wealthy depositors also started to ask for their money and this created what is known as a 'run' on bank deposits. A run happens when depositors lose confidence in the ability of the bank to meet its liabilities and one ends up with depositors queuing up at the bank doors waiting to withdraw their deposits. This phenomenon was demonstrated clearly in early 2008 with the 'run' on the British bank Northern Rock. This run was caused by what has been called 'the credit crunch' where banks in the US, UK and other countries stopped lending to one another. Hence Northern Rock ended up with a liquidity crisis although it was asset rich. In the end the British Government and Bank of England had to step in, inject capital and underwrite the bank.

Europeans invade the world

Large volumes of credit had become integral to European economic expansion so instead of outlawing lending against non-existent deposits i.e. inventing money, a limit was placed on the extent of fictional money that could be created. This new wheeze was called the 'Fractional Reserve System'. So for example; a bank might lend (create) $9 for every $1 it has on deposit. In order to manage this system of phantom money, procedures were put in place for a regime of unannounced inspections so that banks kept to the limits. This system was managed by Central Banks which were created to oversee private banks and to loan money to individual banks in the cases where there was a run on a bank.

This system would sometimes run into difficulties when there was a run on a lot of banks simultaneously.

Fast Forward to Today

The Fractional Reserve System is now the dominant system in the world today.

In the past a paper dollar was a receipt that could be redeemed for a fixed weight of gold or silver. Hence the words "..payable in silver.." used to be printed on a US dollar.

Today a paper or digital dollar can only be redeemed for another paper or digital dollar i.e. "..Federal Reserve Note.." as printed on a contemporary dollar.

It is in this way that money came to represent debt.

In the past private bank credit existed in the form of bank credits that could be refused just as we can refuse a personal cheque today.

Today, private bank credits can be redeemed into Government created 'Fiat Currency'. Fiat currency is money created by a Government order or decree. Fiat literally means in Latin = let it be done (Oxford paperback dictionary 1995: 294). Citizens must accept this money as payment for debts or courts will not enforce judgements.

How much money exists?

In the past the total amount of money in existence was limited to the total amount of the material used as currency i.e. if gold was used to create more money, one could only increase the amount of money in circulation by increasing the amount of gold mined and refined.

Today, money is literally created as debt. New money is created whenever anyone takes out a loan/debt. Therefore the total amount of money created today is limited only by the total amount of new debt created.

In 1957 the total US debt (Corporate, personal, Government) was $5 trillion. In 2006 this figure had risen to $45 trillion.

Remember our old friend, the Fractional Reserve Requirements. Well, these rules to limit the creation of new money have varied from country to country and from time to time i.e. there are no rules that are set in stone. In the past there was $1 of gold held in reserves for every $10 of lending money created. These rules no longer apply and the fractional ratios are now applied to new debt money created on the basis of the old debt money on deposit in banks! What does this mean?

Bank Reserves = Amount of government issued cash + Existing debt money bank has on deposit

Or equivalent deposited at Central Bank

Through this process of fractional lending £1111.12 deposited in a bank becomes £10,000 if a 1:9 ratio is applied. The extra money is simply created by computer with the bank crediting the borrower with £10,000 in their account. Through this multiplication process which is applied to bank lending but not deposits, for every £1111.12 deposited £100,000 of new debt money can be created.

Banks must show they have 10% more on deposit than in loans. This is an illusion. Most people think that loans come out of deposits. This is misleading.

Let's walk through this process:

Step 1
Deposits of £1111.12 turned into lending capacity of £10,000 by fractional reserve lending ratio of 9:1.
£10,000 lent to Ade who wants to buy a car.

Step 2
Ade buys his shiny car and the seller deposits the £10,000 in the bank.
With £1,000 kept on deposit the bank can create a new loan of £9,000

New loan	Reserve
£9,000	£1,000

Step 3
New £9,000 ends up being deposited in a bank after transaction. £900 is left on deposit and a new loan of £8,100 is created:

New loan	Reserve
£8,100	£900

This process continues with the new loan being issued diminishing by 10% each time as follows:

New loan £	Reserve £	Total Money created £
9000	1000	19000
8100	900	27100
7290	810	34390
6560	730	40950
5905	655	46855
etc.	Etc.	etc.
97		99130

£1111.12 x 90 = £100,000 and the bank collects interest on almost £99,000 it never had.

In some countries there is no requirement to make deposits at the Federal Reserve and in other cases Fractional Reserve Ratios are much higher than 9:1 sometimes 20:1 or even 30:1 in some cases.

In effect banks can create as much money as we can borrow.

"Everyone sub-consciously knows banks do not lend money. When you draw on your savings account, the bank doesn't tell you; you can't do this because it has lent the money to somebody else."

Mark Mansfield – economist and author

Of the money that is circulating today only around 5% of it is Government created whilst 95% is from bank credits which are based on the pledges of indebtedness we create when we sign for loans. The amount of the loan (Principal) is created from the borrower's promise to pay. When the principal is repaid i.e. the loan repaid the loan is 'uncreated' and ceases to exist as money.

"I am afraid that the ordinary citizen will not be told that banks can and do create money. ...And they who control the credit of the nation direct the policy of Governments and hold in the hollow of their hands the destiny of the people."

Reginald McKenna – past Chairman of the Board, Midlands Bank of England

The Governments of the world are complicit in this system of fantasy money created out of debt in four principal ways:

1. Legal tender laws which force the use of national Fiat currency
2. All private bank credits to be paid out in this currency
3. Courts enforce debts
4. Governments work to protect the money system's functionalities and credibility but don't tell the public where the money comes from.

When we sign for a loan the only thing of true value in the whole transaction are the assets we promise to forfeit if we renege on the loan.

A mortgage is a portable, exchangeable and saleable piece of paper. The IOU borrowers promise to pay is a form of money.

"This our national circulating medium is now at the mercy of loan transactions of banks, which lend, not money, but promises to supply money they do not possess."

Irving Fisher, economist and author

Without loan agreements the bank has nothing to lend. Banks do not lend money they create it from debt. How can almost everyone be in debt at the same time?

Perpetual Debt

Banks only create the Principal not money to pay the Interest on loans, so where does this additional money come from. The answer is that the financial system is stuck in a vicious circle where new debt money needs to be created to pay the interest on the old debt money and so on. The truth is that in this system all borrowers will never be able to repay their debts. The equations below sets out the proportion of people who will fulfil their debt obligations and the proportion that will be unable to fulfil their debt:

$P/(P + I)$ will fulfil their loan contract
$I/(P + I)$ will be foreclosed

P = Loan Principal $\qquad$ I = Loan Interest

Given that for some loans, such as mortgages, the interest paid is far greater than the principal, during times of economic crisis when there is a squeeze on the money supply (such as in 2008) there will be a huge spate of repossessions/foreclosures, and that is exactly what took place in 2007 and 2008. In the UK the Labour government and Bank of England were forced to put together a rescue package to refloat the mortgage market and this initially involved injecting £50billion of liquidity (new debt money) into the banking market.

"One thing to realise about our fractional reserve banking system is that, like a child's game of musical chairs, as long as the music is playing, there are no losers."

Andrew Gause, Monetary Historian

One of the most interesting aspects of this continuous injection of debt money into the economy is that according to economists increases in money supply cause inflation unless the volume of trade increases by the same amount as the money supply. So we need to wonder why with money being pumped into the Western economies, flat rates of economic growth and decreasing interest rates (which normally stimulates inflation) there is no hyperinflation? It appears that the 'rules' don't apply to some economies but do to others such as Zimbabwe!

Perpetual Economic Growth

There is a normally unstated, taken for granted, assumption that not only is perpetual year on year economic growth desirable, but also that it is possible. However let's think about this belief.

Perpetual economic growth = perpetual growth in the use of the world's resources

If the economy grows by 3% in 2005 and again by 3% in 2006, the 3% growth in 2006 is bigger than the 3% growth in 2005 since it is 3% of 100% + 3%. In the end this type of year on year growth leads to an exponential growth in the size of the economy over a number of years. Economic growth requires resources, oil, gas, wood, gold, copper etc. Since these are finite resources (we are not growing trees fast enough to replace those being cut down) it is simply not possible for us to continue to use these at our current rate, let alone at ever increasing rates of consumption. Something has to give, something will give and when it does may the Creator help us.

"Anyone who believes exponential growth can go on forever in a finite world is either a madman or an economist."

Kenneth Boulding, economist

There is a need for a different outlook, particularly in the rich world. The emphasis needs to be on sustainability and quality of life. There will also need to be changes in the poor world, however the need to satisfy basic needs such as food and clean water mean that the emphasis will need to be different although sustainable development will have to be central to economic policy.

The question of population will also have to be addressed. Caucasians have used population control, euphemistically renamed as family planning, to mask their desire and intent to suppress and even reduce the population of Afrikans on the Motherland and in 'the West'. Population control has always been closely linked to the eugenics movement, which has focused not only on suppressing the Black and Brown populations of the world but also on preventing those Caucasians who are considered intellectually feeble from reproducing. This latter drive led to the sterilisation and incarceration of thousands of Caucasians in the USA in sanatoriums in the 1920s and '30s as well as the sterilisation of tens of thousands of 'mentally defective' Caucasians in such 'liberal' countries as Canada and Sweden as well as other countries in Europe right up to the 1970's.

The following quote cited in the book 'Missing Assets – Cultural, Psychological and Biological Origins of Infertility' by Keidi Obi Awadu demonstrates European intent towards Afrika and the Southern hemisphere.

"..for population control to succeed, a great deal more must be done than to merely establish family planning centers and to provide surreptitious funding for local advocacy campaigns. An entire spectrum of variables affecting the desire to have children must be influenced – from basic economics and government programs to family relations, personal expectations, lifestyle, cultural tradition, concepts of land sharing and private ownership, wealth production systems, ethical standards, and even religious beliefs. Taboos must be breached, the bonds that unite family and community must be undermined, and sufficient disruption must occur to literally disorient the targeted communities and make them vulnerable to the imposition of external cultural forces."

Awadu, K.O. (Oct 1997) Vol 4, No 5. The Conscious Rasta Press, Long Beach, California

Taking on board and notwithstanding the foregoing analysis Afrikan leaders need to assess how many people their countries can sustainably support and what happens when that figure is reached. At present Afrika is relatively under populated, as a result of the depredations of the enslavement process, however Afrikan population growth is currently very strong and therefore this situation needs to be reviewed not just for today and tomorrow, but for 20, 40, 100 years into the future.

If we return to the question of the role of governments in this financial conspiracy there are four questions that point to their complicity:

1. Why do governments *choose* to borrow money from private banks at interest when government could create all the interest free money it needs itself?
2. Why create money as debt? Why not create money that circulates permanently?
3. How can a money system dependent on perpetually accelerating growth be used to build a sustainable economy?
4. Why is the current system dependent upon perpetual growth?

Usury – A very interesting subject

At one time charging any interest on a loan was called usury (today, in the European financial system, the term is usually only applied to the charging of very high interest rates) and the penalty was severe and could even be death. Many religions (including Judaism, Christianity and Islam) forbade usury on moral grounds. However over time the counterargument that lending money involves risk and what they call 'opportunity cost', won out in the 'Western' financial system and usury has spread around the world.

Charging interest is both a moral and practical problem. Money lenders end up with all the money.

"I have never yet had anyone who could through the use of logic and reason justify the Federal Government borrowing the use of its own money… I believe the time will come when people will demand that this be changed. I believe the time will come in this country when they will actually blame you, me and everyone else connected with the Congress for sitting idly by and permitting such an idiotic system to continue."

Wright Patman, Democratic Congressman 1928 – 1976
Chairman, Committee on Banking and Currency 1963-1975

Alternative Systems

Money is just an IDEA. It is represented as:

- Symbol
- Commodity
- Receipt for commodity
- Bogus receipt
- Fiat (Government cash)
- Debt (Bank credit)
- Debt (Pledge)

In the past there have been alternative systems of money which worked well which were destroyed by bankers and their allies. Let's take a look at a couple.

Tally Stick System

The following information was taken from the blog Money 101 (posted Friday 13 January 2006) *http://wakeupfromyourslumber.blogspot.com/2006/01/money-101.html*

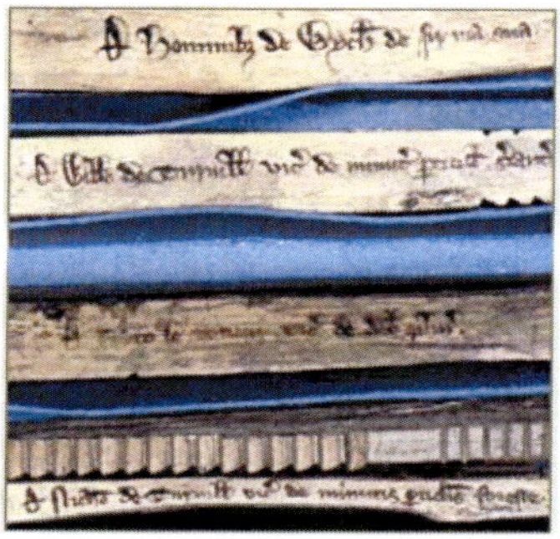

At the top is an image of King Henry the First's tally stick:

THE TALLY STICKS (1100-1854) King Henry the First produced sticks of polished wood, with notches cut along one edge to signify the denominations. The stick was then split full length so each piece still had a record of the notches.

The King kept one half for proof against counterfeiting, and then spent the other half into the market place where it would continue to circulate as money.

Because only Tally Sticks were accepted by Henry for payment of taxes, there was a built in demand for them, which gave people confidence to accept these as money.

He could have used anything really, so long as the people agreed it had value, and **his willingness to accept these sticks as legal tender made it easy for the people to agree. Money is only as valuable as people's faith in it,** and without that faith even today's money is just paper.

The tally stick system worked really well for 726 years. It was the most successful form of currency in recent history and the British Empire was actually built under the Tally Stick system, but how is it that most of us are not aware of its existence?

Perhaps the fact that **in 1694 the Bank of England at its formation attacked the Tally Stick System** gives us a clue as to why most of us have never heard of them. They realised **it was money outside the power of the money changers,** (the very thing King Henry had intended).

Colonial Scrips

http://reactor-core.org/america-created-money.html

AMERICA CREATED ITS OWN MONEY IN 1750

How Benjamin Franklin Made New England Prosperous

Copyright © 1941 by Congressman Charles G. Binderup

The following historical story is taken from a radio address given by Congressman Charles G. Binderup of Nebraska, some 50 years ago and was reprinted in Unrobing the Ghosts of Wall Street:

Colonies More Prosperous Than The Home Country

Before the American War for Independence in 1776, the colonized part of what is today the United States of America was a possession of England. It was called New England, and was made up of 13 colonies, which became the first 13 states of the great Republic. Around 1750, this New England was very prosperous. Benjamin Franklin was able to write:

"There was abundance in the Colonies, and peace was reigning on every border. It was difficult, and even impossible, to find a happier and more prosperous nation on all the surface of the globe. Comfort was prevailing in every home. The people, in general, kept the highest moral standards, and education was widely spread."

When Benjamin Franklin went over to England to represent the interests of the Colonies, he saw a completely different situation: the working population of this country was gnawed by hunger and poverty. "The streets are covered with beggars and tramps," he wrote. He asked his English friends how England, with all its wealth, could have so much poverty among its working classes.

His friends replied that England was a prey to a terrible condition: it had too many workers! The rich said they were already overburdened with taxes, and could not pay more to relieve the needs and poverty of this mass of workers. Several rich Englishmen of that time actually believed, along with Malthus, that wars and plague were necessary to rid the country from man-power surpluses.

Franklin's friends then asked him how the American Colonies managed to collect enough money to support their poor houses, and how they could overcome this plague of pauperism. Franklin replied:

"We have no poor houses in the Colonies; and if we had some, there would be nobody to put in them, since there is, in the Colonies, not a single unemployed person, neither beggars nor tramps."

Thanks To Free Money Issued By The Nation

His friends could not believe their ears, and even less understand this fact, since when the English poor houses and jails became too cluttered, England shipped these poor wretches and down-and- outs, like cattle, and discharged, on the quays of the Colonies, those who had survived the poverty, dirtiness and privations of the journey. At that time, England was throwing into jail those who could not pay their debts. They therefore asked Franklin how he could explain the remarkable prosperity of the New England Colonies. Franklin replied:

"That is simple. In the Colonies, we issue our own paper money. It is called 'Colonial Scrip.' We issue it in proper proportion to make the goods and pass easily from the producers to the consumers. ***In this manner, creating ourselves our own paper money, we control its purchasing power and we have no interest to pay to no one."***

The Bankers Impose Poverty

The information came to the knowledge of the English Bankers, and held their attention. They immediately took the necessary steps to have the British Parliament to pass a law that prohibited the Colonies from using their scrip money, and then ordered them to use only the gold and silver money that was provided in sufficient quantity by the English bankers. **Then began in America the plague of debt-money,**

which has never since brought so many curses to the American people.

The first law was passed in 1751, and then completed by a more restrictive law in 1763. Franklin reported that one year after the implementation of this prohibition on Colonial money, the streets of the Colonies were filled with unemployment and beggars, just like in England, because there was not enough money to pay for the goods and work. The circulating medium of exchange had been reduced by half.

Franklin added that this was the original cause of the American Revolution - and not the tax on tea nor the Stamp Act, as it has been taught again and again in history books. The financiers always manage to have removed from school books all that can throw light on their own schemes, and damage the glow that protects their power.

Franklin, who was one of the chief architects of the American independence, wrote it clearly:

"The Colonies would gladly have borne the little tax on tea and other matters had it not been the poverty caused by the bad influence of the English bankers on the Parliament, which has caused in the Colonies hatred of England and the Revolutionary War."

This point of view of Franklin was confirmed by great statesmen of his era: John Adams, Jefferson, and several others. A remarkable English historian, John Twells, wrote, speaking of the money of the Colonies, the Colonial Scrip:

"It was the monetary system under which America's Colonies flourished to such an extent that Edmund Burke was able to write about them: 'Nothing in the history of the world resembles their progress. It was a sound and beneficial system, and its effects led to the happiness of the people.'" John Twells adds:

"In a bad hour, the British Parliament took away from America its representative money, forbade any further issue of bills of credit, these bills ceasing to be legal tender, and ordered that all taxes should be paid in coins. Consider now the consequences: this restriction of the medium of exchange paralyzed all the industrial energies of the people. Ruin took place in these once flourishing Colonies; most rigorous distress visited every family and every business, discontent

became desperation, and reached a point, to use the words of Dr. Johnson, when human nature rises up and asserts its rights."

Another writer, Peter Cooper, expresses himself along the same lines. After having said how Franklin had explained to the London Parliament the cause of the prosperity of the Colonies, he wrote:

"After Franklin gave explanations on the true cause of the prosperity of the Colonies, the Parliament exacted laws forbidding the use of this money in the payment of taxes. This decision brought so many drawbacks and so much poverty to the people that it was the main cause of the Revolution. The suppression of the Colonial money was a much more important reason for the general uprising than the Tea and Stamp Act."

Today, in America as well as in Europe, we are under the regime of the Scrip of the Bankers instead of the scrip of the nation. Hence the public debts, everlasting interest charges, taxes that plunder purchasing power, with the only result being a consolidation of the financial dictatorship.

"The inability of the Colonialists to get power to issue their own money permanently out of the hands of George III and the International bankers was the PRIME reason for the revolutionary war." *Benjamin Franklin*

So, we have seen that there were money systems that worked well without creating perpetually increasing debt.

The death knell for ordinary US citizens and final triumph for bankers was when in 1913 President Woodrow Wilson signed into effect the Federal Reserve Act which put the international Banking cartel in charge of creating US money. This was an act that Wilson would later bitterly regret as he lamented:

"I am a most unhappy man. I have unwillingly ruined my country. A good industrial nation is controlled by its system of credit. Our system of credit is concentrated. The growth of the nation, therefore and all our activities are in the hands of a few men. We have come to be one of the worst ruled, one of the most completely controlled and dominated Governments in the civilised world, no longer a Government by free opinion...no longer a Government by conviction and the majority, but a Government by the opinion and desire of a small group of dominant men."

I listened to a radio broadcast on BBC Five Live on 30 April 2008 when a writer was promoting his book on the super elite, the 6000 or so people whom he has identified as playing a major role in determining world affairs. Many years ago David Rockerfeller spoke to his fellow members of this group.

"We are grateful to the Washington Post, the New York Times, Time magazine and other great publications whose Directors have attended our meetings and respected the promises of discretion for almost forty years. It would have been almost impossible for us to develop our plan for the world if we had been subject to the bright lights of publicity during those years. But the world is now more sophisticated and prepared to march towards a world government. The supranational sovereignty of an intellectual elite and world bankers is surely preferable to the National auto-determination practiced in past centuries."

David Rockerfeller in address to Trilateral Commission meeting in 1991

Permanent Interest Free Money

What the foregoing is suggesting is that money should be created as Value (roads, railways, schools, solar panels etc.) and not as Debt.

The increases in the stock market and the housing markets are just as much part of inflation as increases in bread prices. What that means is that increasing the money supply benefits the rich most of all. It moves money from those who use cash to those who own assets (shares, property etc). That is, inflation moves money from the poor to the rich.

Inflation = a flat Tax on money and spending power. For example if you have £100 and inflation is 20% per annum, after one year your £100 will have the equivalent buying power of £80.

In a saner financial world governments alone would create money and they would work to preserve the value of that money. There would be no tax money paid out on interest, because government would not be borrowing their own money from private banks. Hence there would be no national debt. The following quotes reinforce the reality of financial slavery that rules the Earth.

"Money is a new form of slavery, and distinguishable from the old form simply by the fact that it is imperial, there is no human relation between nation and slave." *Leo Tolstoy*

"None are more enslaved than those who falsely believe they are free." *Goethe*

"The modern banking system manufactures money out of nothing. The process is perhaps the most astounding piece of sleight of hand that was ever invented. Banking was conceived in iniquity and born in sin. Bankers own the Earth. Take it away from them, but leave them the power to create money and with the flick of a pen they will create enough money to buy it back again....Take this great power away from them and all great fortunes like mine will disappear and they ought to disappear, for then this would be a better and happier world to live in. But if you want to continue to be the slaves of the banks and pay the costs of your own slavery, then let bankers continue to create money and control credit."

Sir Josiah Stamp – Director, Bank of England 1928-1941 (reputed to be the second richest man in England at the time of the quote)

THE CREDIT CRUNCH, BAILOUT AND OTHER DECEPTIONS EXPLAINED

Introduction

If there is ever to be hope of achieving global economic justice it is vital that as many people as possible are made aware of the gross economic manipulation and fraud being perpetrated by the economic elite. Once awareness has been raised we then face the enormous task of organising people of goodwill to overthrow this system of economic slavery that has the majority of the world's population in financial chains.

In this chapter I will provide you with an overview of the widely reported causes of the financial crisis of 2008 along with an explanation of the more deep rooted, systemic causes, some of which were touched upon in the earlier chapter on 'Money, Debt, Interest and Bankers'. There is extensive coverage given to the manipulation of government economic data since this is one of the major ways in which governments maintain the public's confidence in the economic system and convince people the economy is growing when it is contracting, that inflation is low when it is high and that unemployment is at historically low levels when in fact it is very high. We are going to pull back the curtain to show you the real face of the Wizard of Oz and his tools of manipulation and control.

The Great Credit Crunch Hoax

In January 2009 just as I thought I had finally finished this book I came across an article by Robert Higgs which asserted that the credit crunch was to all intents and purposes – and certainly as it related to inter-bank lending in the US, where the whole mess originated - a hoax. When I saw the title of his short article 'The Great Credit Crunch Hoax of 2008' I was intrigued. However the single graph contained in the article was enough to convince me that he was on to something and that once again the vast majority of us had been had, hoodwinked, deceived, conned, bamboozled and plain tricked. Higgs tells us:

"....I am rather embarrassed, on behalf of all these giants of the ruling elite, to inform you that in retrospect the Monster from Lack-of-Liquidity Lagoon doesn't really show up as such in the most relevant statistical series.

Probably the most important measure of credit-market conditions is the amount of commercial-bank credit outstanding. These ***figures*** show that although the middle part of 2008 does stand out in the long view, it does so not by virtue of credit's frightening contraction, but only by virtue of its hitting a ***six-month plateau*** from April through September.

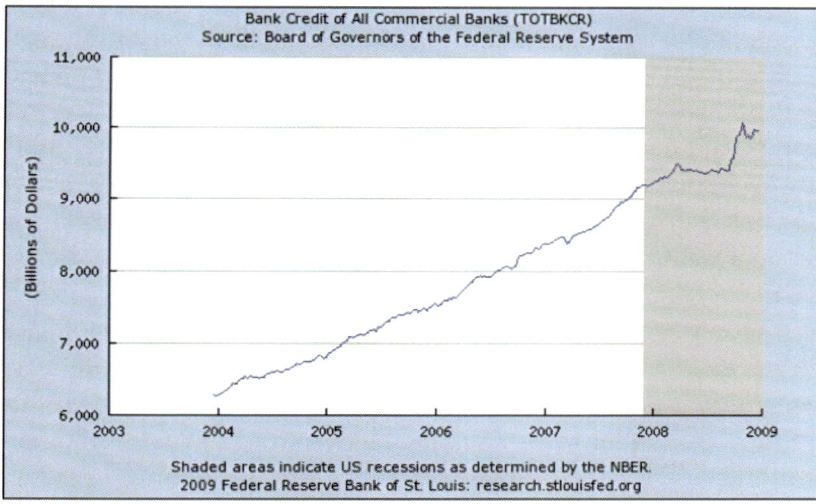

At no time during that interval, however, did the amount of commercial-bank credit outstanding fall below the amount outstanding at the beginning of the year. In short, credit was actually ample, indeed, at an all-time high; it simply stopped growing as usual for six months, stuck at about $9.4 trillion, while one Wall Street wizard after another told NPR that "no money is moving, the credit market is completely shut down" or some such cock-and-bull story.

After the six-month pause, commercial-bank credit zipped upward again, so that by the end of the year, the amount outstanding stood more than 8 percent higher than it had a year earlier. Some credit crunch! Année terrible, indeed.

But don't write off this silly little hoax too fast, because, however baseless it might have been in economic reality, it was manifestly good enough for government work. And that work has now placed U.S. taxpayers on the hook for trillions of dollars of additional ***Treasury commitments*** and put all holders of ***U.S. dollars*** and other dollar-denominated assets at risk of tremendous losses of their money's purchasing power.

The beauty of the Great Hoax of 2008, from the perspective of the ruling class, is that it was also a Great Scare, and such scares invariably serve as ***pretexts*** for the rulers' most audacious assaults on the peasants' lives, liberties, and purses. You'd almost have to admire the elite's ability to spook the rest of us into blind, unreasoning panic on such a flimsy basis, if it weren't for the fact that after the episode has passed, we find ourselves enormously worse off, our economic prospects diminished greatly and our liberties throttled more tightly by an even bigger Leviathan, with nothing to show for it on the upside but the further enrichment of a handful of big bankers and other malefactors of great wealth and power..." *http://www.lewrockwell.com/higgs/higgs102.html*

So there you have it. Financial institutions which were hugely overleveraged (high debt:asset ratios) were able to offload 'toxic assets' onto the hapless taxpayer and further consolidate the corporate cartels that run the financial sector and by extension have huge influence over the functioning of the world economy.

The 2008 US Bailout

In seeking to provide the reader with an explanation for what really caused the global financial crisis of 2008 I thought I would start with the views of a former insider and true believer in the system of global corporate capitalism. Paul Craig Roberts was Assistant Secretary of the Treasury in the Reagan administration. He was Associate Editor of the Wall Street Journal editorial page and Contributing Editor of National Review. His articles are published in many publications and websites and make interesting reading. When reading the following extracts bear in mind his not unnatural tendency to defend the record of the Reagan administration of which he was a part. We should not forget that Reaganomics brought misery to millions of poor people in the US and involved the transfer of wealth to the economic elite under the system of corporate welfare that is the norm in the US.

In writing on the US government's financial rescue package he highlights a number of inconsistencies in their strategy which indicate that the stated aims of this intervention were not the real motivations driving government action.

"Just as the Bush regime's wars have been used to pour billions of dollars into the pockets of its military-security donor base, the Paulson bailout looks like a Bush regime scheme to incur $700 billion in new public debt in order to transfer the money into the coffers of its financial donor base. The US taxpayers will be left with the interest payments in perpetuity (or inflation if the Fed monetizes the debt), and the number of Wall Street billionaires will grow. As for the US and European governments' purchases of bank shares, that is just a cover for funnelling public money into private hands.

The explanations that have been given for the crisis and its bailout are opaque. The US Treasury estimates that as few as 7% of the mortgages are bad. Why then do the US, UK, Germany, and France need to pour more than $2.1 trillion of public money into private financial institutions?

If, as the government tells us, the crisis stems from subprime mortgage defaults reducing the interest payments to the holders of mortgage backed securities, thus driving down their values and threatening the solvency of the institutions that hold them, why isn't the bailout money used to address the problem at its source? If the bailout money was used to refinance troubled mortgages and to pay off foreclosed mortgages, the mortgage backed securities would be made whole, and it would be unnecessary to pour huge sums of public money into banks. Instead, the bailout money is being used to inject capital into financial institutions and to purchase from them troubled financial instruments.

It is a strange solution that does not address the problem. As the US economy sinks deeper into recession, the mortgage defaults will rise. Thus, the problem will intensify, necessitating the purchase of yet more troubled instruments.

If credit card debt has also been securitized and sold as investments, as the economy worsens defaults on credit card debt will be a replay of the mortgage defaults. How much debt can the Treasury bail out before its own credit rating sinks?

The bailout package is a result of panic and threats, not of analysis and understanding. Neither Congress nor the public knows the full story. If the problem is the mortgages, why does the bailout leave the mortgages unaddressed and focus instead on pouring vast amount of public money into private financial institutions?

The purpose of regulation is to restrain greed and to prevent leveraged speculation from threatening the wider society. Congress needs to restore financial regulation, not reward those who caused the crisis." '*Additional Thoughts on the Bailout*' October 16, 2008 www.Information Clearinghouse.com

In an earlier article entitled '*A Futile Bailout As Darkness Falls On America*' Roberts identifies the timescale and chief culprits involved in the deregulation of the banking and financial system that he believes led to the financial collapse of 2008.

"America has become a pretty discouraging place. Americans, for the most part, will never know what happened to them, because they no longer have a free and responsible press. They have Big Brother's press. For example, on September 28, 2008, a New York Times editorial blamed the current financial crisis on "antiregulation disciples of the Reagan Revolution."

What utter nonsense. Every example of deregulation that the New York Times editorial provides is located in the Clinton Administration and the George W. Bush administration. I was a member of the Reagan administration. We most certainly did not deregulate the financial system.

The repeal of the Glass-Steagall Act, which separated commercial from investment banking, was the achievement of the Democratic Clinton Administration. It happened in 1999, over a decade after Reagan left office.

It was in 2000 that derivatives and credit default swaps were excluded from regulation.

The greatest mistake was made in 2004, the year that Reagan died.

That year the current Secretary of the Treasury, Henry M. Paulson Jr, was head of the investment bank Goldman Sachs. In the spring of 2004, the investment banks, led by Paulson, met with the Securities and Exchange Commission. At this meeting with the New Deal regulatory agency tasked with regulating the US financial system, Paulson convinced the SEC Commissioners to exempt the investment banks from maintaining reserves to cover losses on investments. The exemption granted by the SEC allowed the investment banks to leverage financial instruments beyond any bounds of prudence.

In place of time-proven standards of prudence, computer models engineered by hot shots determined acceptable risk. As one result Bear Stearns, for example, pushed its leverage ratio to 33 to 1. For every one dollar in equity, the investment bank had $33 of debt!

It was computer models that led to the failure of Long-Term Capital Management in 1998, the first systemic threat to the financial system. Why the SEC went along with Paulson and set aside capital requirements after the scare of Long-Term Capital Management is inexplicable.

The blame is headed toward SEC chairman Christopher Cox. This is more of Big Brother's disinformation. Cox, like so many others, was a victim of a free market ideology, itself a reaction to over-regulation, that was boosted by academic economic opinion, rewarded with Nobel prizes, that the market "always knows best".

The Paulson bailout saves his firm, Goldman Sachs. The Paulson bailout transfers the troubled financial instruments that the financial sector created from the books of the financial sector to the books of the taxpayers at the US Treasury. This is all the bailout does. It rescues the guilty. The Paulson bailout does not address the problem, which is the defaulting home mortgages.

The defaults will continue, because the economy is sinking into recession. Homeowners are losing their jobs, and homeowners are being hit with rising mortgage payments resulting from adjustable rate mortgages and escalator interest rate clauses in their mortgages that make homeowners unable to service their debt.

Shifting the troubled assets from the financial sectors' books to the taxpayers' books absolves the people who caused the problem from responsibility. As the economy declines and mortgage default rates rise, the US Treasury and the American taxpayers could end up with a $700 billion loss.

If the $700 billion bailout is based on an estimate of the current amount of bad mortgages, as the recession deepens and Americans lose their jobs, the default rate will rise. The $700 billion might not suffice. The Treasury will have to go hat in hand to its foreign creditors for more loans.

As the US Treasury has not got $7, much less $700 billion, it must borrow the bailout money from foreign creditors, already overloaded with US paper. At what point do America's foreign bankers decide that the additions to US debt exceed what can be repaid?

This question was ignored by the bailout. There were no hearings. No one consulted China, America's principal banker, or the Japanese, or the OPEC sovereign wealth funds, or Europe.

Does the world have a blank check for America's mistakes?

This is the same world that is faced with American demands that countries support with money and lives America's quest for world hegemony. Europeans are dying in Afghanistan for American hegemony. Do Europeans want their banks, which hold US dollars as their reserves, to fail so that Paulson can bail out his company and his friends?

The US dollar is the world's reserve currency. It comprises the reserves of foreign central banks. Bush's wars and economic policies are destroying the basis of the US dollar as reserve currency. The day the dollar loses its reserve currency role, the US government cannot pay its bills in its own currency. The result will be a dramatic reduction in US living standards.

Currently Treasuries are boosted by the habitual "flight to quality," but as Treasury debt deepens, will investors still see quality? At what point do America's foreign creditors cease to lend? That is the point at which American power ends. It might be close at hand.

The Paulson bailout is predicated on cleaning up financial institutions' balance sheets and restoring the flow of credit. The assumption is that once lending resumes, the economy will pick up. This assumption is problematic. The expansion of consumer debt, which kept the economy going in the 21st century, has reached its limit. There are no more credit cards to max out, and no more home equity to refinance and spend. The Paulson bailout might restore trust among financial institutions and enable them to lend to one another, but it doesn't provide a jolt to consumer demand.

Moreover, there may be more shoes to drop. Credit card debt could be the next to threaten balance sheets of financial institutions. Apparently, credit card debt has been securitized and sold as well, and not all of the debt is good..

According to statistician John Williams [*http://www.shadowstats.com/section/commentaries*] who measures inflation, unemployment, and GDP according to the methodology used prior to the Clinton regime's corruption of these measures, the US unemployment rate is currently at 14.7 per cent and the inflation rate is 13.2 per cent. Consequently, real US GDP growth in the 21st century has been negative...

Some commentators are blaming the current mortgage problem on the pressure that the US government put on banks to lend to unqualified borrowers. However, whatever breaches of prudence there may have been only affected the earnings of individual institutions. They did not threaten the financial system. The current crisis required more than bad loans. It required securitization and its leverage. It required Fed chairman Alan Greenspan's inappropriate low interest rates, which created a real estate boom. Rapidly rising real estate prices quickly created home equity to justify 100 percent mortgages. Wall Street analysts pushed financial companies to improve their bottom lines, which they did by extreme leveraging. .

The same reckless leadership that gave us expensive wars based on false premises has now concocted an expensive bailout that does not address the problem, which will fester and become worse." Paul Craig Roberts 8 October, 2008, **Counterpunch** in *www.countercurrents.org*

Roberts is an 'insider' who provides a good explanation of the economic crisis of 2008 from the perspective of a 'believer' in the capitalistic economic system as constructed by the USA and its allies. His desire is for modification, and some more regulation of the current system. No doubt the maintenance of some of the regulatory and restrictive measures that were removed between 1999 and 2004 would have prevented or ameliorated the effects of the current crisis, however one should bear in mind that boom and bust and these types of economic crises stemming from problems in the financial markets have been a regular, cyclical occurrence in the history of corporate' capitalism and indeed can be said to be inherent to and an integral component of the operation of these financial markets.

He is not alone amongst insiders who recognise the insanity of trying to use the creation of more debt to solve a problem caused by exponentially rising levels of indebtedness.

Michael Hudson is a former Wall Street economist. He was Dennis Kucinich's Chief Economic Advisor in the recent Democratic primary presidential campaign, and has advised the U.S., Canadian, Mexican and Latvian governments, as well as the United Nations Institute for Training and Research (UNITAR). He is a Distinguished Research Professor at the University of Missouri, Kansas City. His analysis shows why Kucinich was almost certainly the best of the Democratic candidates for the US Presidency, and hence why he was doomed to defeat from the outset.

In his article he reinforces the unsustainable nature of the money as debt financial system described earlier in this book.

"Banks cannot make money *ad infinitum* by selling more and more credit – that is, indebting the non-financial economy more and more. Government officials such as Treasury Secretary Paulson or Federal Reserve Chairman Bernanke are professionally unable to acknowledge this problem, and it does not appear in most neoclassical or monetarist textbooks. But the underlying mathematics of compound interest are rediscovered in each generation, often prompted by the force majeur of financial crisis.

A generation ago, for instance, Hyman Minsky gained a following by describing what he aptly called the Ponzi stage of the business cycle. It was the phase in which debtors no longer were able to pay off their loans out of current income (as in Stage #1, where they earned enough to cover their interest and amortization charges), and indeed did not even earn enough to pay the interest charges (as in

Stage #2), but had to borrow the money to pay the interest owed to their bankers and other creditors. In this Stage #3 the interest was simply added onto the debt, growing at a compound rate. It ends in a crash."

Hudson goes on to describe the underlying problem with interest charges which I also highlighted earlier. Whilst interest seems great – and is great in a narrow self-centred view – for those levying or receiving the interest, in the end it acts as a tax on real economic productivity and impoverishes more people than it enriches. Hudson tells us that:

"This was the flip side of the magic of compound interest – the belief that people can get rich by "putting money to work". Money doesn't really work, of course. When lent out, it extracts interest from the "real" production and consumption economy, that is, from the labor and industry that actually do the work. It is much like a tax, a monopoly rent levied by the financial sector. Yet this quasi-tax, this extractive financial rent (as Alfred Marshall explained over a century ago) is the dynamic that is supposed to enable corporate, state and local pension funds to pay for retirement simply out of stock market gains and bond investments – purely financially and hence at the expense of the economy at large whose employees are supposed to be gainers. This is the essence of "pension-fund capitalism," a Ponzi-scheme variant of finance capitalism. Unfortunately, it is grounded in purely mathematical relationships that have little grounding in the "real" economy in which families and companies produce and consume"...

Hudson describes how by acting as financial good Samaritan for the financial institutions the US government has loaded an enormous weight of debt on ordinary US taxpayers.

"By increasing America's national debt from $5 trillion earlier this year to $13 trillion in almost a single swoop by taking on junk loans and other bad investments rather than letting them go under as traditionally has occurred in the "cleansing" culmination of business crashes ("cleansing" in the sense of clean slates for debts that cannot reasonably be paid), Paulson's bailout actions increase the interest payments that the government must pay out of taxes or by borrowing (or printing) yet more money. Someone must pay for bad debts and junk loans that are not wiped off the books. The government is now to take on the roll of debt collector to "make a profit for taxpayers" by going around and kneecapping the economy – which of course is comprised primarily of the "taxpayers" ostensibly being helped."

It should be noted that David Walker former Comptroller General (US) – this means he was head of the government accounting office – for ten years from 1998 estimates the total US national debt is $55,000,000,000,000 ($55 trillion) or $480,000 per US household as of 2008. You can view his interview with Bill Maher at the following site *http://www.youtube.com/watch?v=0NM5Q5VDpnA*. He has also made a documentary on this subject *IOUSA*.

Michael Hudson goes on to describe this use of interest to squeeze the 'real economy'. He also provides an interesting 2141 year historical precedent for the current financial crisis which just goes to prove that these types of crisis are systemic to this type of debt based economy.

"It is a con game. Financial gains have soared since 1980, but banks and institutional investors have not used them to finance tangible capital formation. They simply have recycled their receipt of interest (and credit-card fees and penalties that often amount to as much as interest) into yet new loans, extracting yet more interest and so on. This financial extraction leaves less personal and business income to spend on consumer goods, capital goods and services. Sales shrink, causing defaults as the economy is less able to pay its stipulated interest charges.

This phenomenon of debt deflation has occurred throughout history, not only over the modern business cycle but for centuries at a time. The most self-destructive example of financial short-termism is the decline and fall of the Roman Empire into debt bondage and ultimately into a Dark Age. The political turning point was the violent takeover of the Senate by oligarchic creditors who murdered the debtor-oriented reformers led by the Gracchi brothers in 133 BC, picking up benches and using them as rams to push the reformers over the cliff on which the political assembly was located. A similar violent overthrow occurred in Sparta a century earlier when its kings Agis and Cleomenes sought to annul debts so as to reverse the city-state's economic polarization. The creditor oligarchy exiled and killed the kings, as Plutarch described in his Parallel Lives of the Illustrious Greeks and Romans. This used to be basic reading among educated people, but today these events have all but disappeared from most people's historical memory. A knowledge of the evolution of economic structures has been replaced by a mere series of political personalities and military conquests."

The only temporary solution is debt deflation, i.e. wiping out a significant portion of the crippling mountain of debt.

"This attempt is necessarily in vain. No amount of money can sustain the exponential growth of debt, not to mention the freely created credit and mutual gambles on derivatives and other financial claims whose volume has exploded in recent years. The government is committed to 'bailing out' banks and other creditors whose loans and swaps have gone bad. It remains in denial with regard to the debt deflation that must be imposed on the rest of the economy to 'make good' on these financial trends.

"Here's why the plan for the government to recover the money is whistling in the dark: It calls for banks to 'earn their way out of debt' by selling more of their product – credit, that is, debt. Homeowners and other consumers, students and car buyers, credit card users and their employers – the 'taxpayers' supposed to be helped – are to pay the repayment money to the banks, instead of using it to purchase goods and services. If they charge only 6 per cent per year, they will extract $93 billion in interest charges – $42 billion to pay the Treasury for its $700 billion, and another $51 billion for the Federal Reserve's $850 billion in 'cash for trash' loans."

Hudson concludes by reinforcing the collusion between Wall Street and both the Republicans and Democrats which means that whoever is notionally in power it is always business as usual.

"The problem of 'debt pollution' is being 'solved' by creating yet more debt, not by reducing its volume. Neither the Treasury nor Congress is helping to resolve this problem. The working assumption is that giving newly created government debt to the banks and Wall Street will lead to more lending to re-inflate the real estate and stock markets. But who will lend more to the one-sixth of U.S. homes already said to have fallen into negative equity territory? As debt deflation eats into the domestic market for goods and services, corporate sales and earnings will shrink, dragging down stock prices. Wall Street is in control, but its policies are so shortsighted that they are eroding the underlying economy – which is passing from democracy to oligarchy, and indeed it seems to a bipartisan financial kleptocracy."

Source: *Licensed Kleptocracy for Years to Come The ABCs of Paulson's Bailout*, by Michael Hudson October 21, 2008 "Counterpunch" *http://www.informationclearinghouse.info/article21066.htm*

The 2009 Obama Bailouts – Continue to bend over and grit your teeth

Buying into the Obama myth – Unfortunately the majority of Afrikans and many people from other 'racial' groups continue to imbibe Obama juice - a highly intoxicating substance so it seems – on a daily basis and hence steadfastly refuse to engage in any serious analysis of his political policies or allegiances. Hence the Wall Street candidate remains clothed in his sheepskin 'man of the people' cloak. Supporting Obama has almost become a point of principle, or act of faith; for Obamaholics and woe betide people such as me who dare to move beyond emotionalism to embrace analysis or reject symbolism in favour of substance. We are, as the comedian Billy Connolly once remarked, about as welcome as a fart in an astronaut's suit, when it comes to discussions of the President of the United States by his devotees.

Well, if you have read my previous books you will guess that the more the Obamaites froth with indignation at the suggestion that this is not the supreme culmination of Afrikan people's struggle, in the US and elsewhere, against oppression and subjugation; the more I feel inclined to present information, analysis and opinions to counter this check your brain in at the cloakroom and go into the hall to clap, sing and get happy, nonsense. My website *www.houseofknowledge.org.uk* deals with Obama's wider policy positions and others such as Glen

Ford of Black Agenda Report have thoroughly analysed Obama's politics, his position vis a vis Afrikans in the US and the incredible contradiction of those Black Nationalists who strongly support Obama whilst vociferously criticising the US government's policies on a myriad of issues such as Zimbabwe – which they decry as crimes against humanity or war crimes – all of which were supported by Obama prior to his election and all of which continue to be implemented by him as President.

Most of the debates on the Obama phenomenon that I have listened to, or observed, have been quite frankly embarrassing. To see highly intelligent Afrikan scholars and activists who normally come to debates armed with a range of facts and information from an array of sources; reduced to building an argument for supporting Obama based around ideas such as:

- He is married to a Black woman so that is good enough for me
- He has a beautiful family
- It is a symbolic moment for the world
- We can't expect too much of him
- He will inspire our children
- He plays basketball which is an Afrikan-American sporting preference
- He has an Afrikan name

is enough to make me cringe.

Among the many issues these apologists for Obama almost never discuss in any detail include:

- Why Obama was the No.1 choice of Wall Street, including the huge campaign contributions he received from the financial elites
- Obama's foreign policy positions, particularly in relation to Afrika e.g. Zimbabwe, Somalia, Congo
- Obama's toe-curlingly servile speech to AIPAC, immediately after gaining the democratic nomination -

which even outdid Hillary Clinton and John McCain for bootlicking – and his failure to condemn the numerous Israeli war crimes in Gaza

- His selling out of Black farmers in the US in their fight to gain adequate compensation for years of systematic discrimination in the provision of grants to farmers by the US government's Department of Agriculture
- His administration's $73,000,000 cut in funding for Historically Black Colleges
- Obama's ghoulish team of advisors/cabinet members, made up of large segments of the old Bill Clinton administration, hard-core Zionists, cold-war warriors and Republicans. Not a 'progressive' to be seen anywhere.
- His ardent support for 'Planned Parenthood' (founded by the hard core White Supremacist Margaret Sanger) and their programme of population control/racial elimination aimed at Afrikan women in the US
- His support for the Bush bailout of Wall Street which was just another case of welfare for the rich and that his key economic advisors were either amongst the architects of the economic crisis e.g. Larry Summers and Paul Volcker (who was the Chairman of the Federal Reserve under Jimmy Carter and Ronald Reagan [from August 1979 to August 1987] and is currently chairman of the newly formed Economic Recovery Advisory Board under Barack Obama, member of the Bilderberg Group, Trilateral Commission and Council on Foreign Relations) or protégés of the architects e.g. Timothy Geithner (former President of the New York Federal Reserve, Bilderberg Group and Trilateral Commission) who learned his craft at the side of James Rubin. James Rubin is a devoted Wall Street advocate who was Assistant Secretary of State for Public Affairs and Chief Spokesman for the State Department from 1997 to May 2000 in the Clinton administration and helped push through the

repeal of the Glass Steagell Act in 1999 which was one of the causes of the current financial crisis.

A politician, Cynthia McKinney, who in comparison to Obama, is a committed defender of Afrikan people got to the heart of the Obama deception in an email article 'Ruminations on President Obama's Tenure Thus Far and "Acceptable Punditry" ' distributed in early March 2009. She noted;

"... it is clear that the Obama Administration is continuing the Bush policies for missile strikes inside Pakistan; torture; rendition for torture; public release of Bush Administration e-mails; illegal wiretaps; status of prisoners at the U.S. base in Bagram, Afghanistan; and workplace immigration raids?

For the record, President Obama is also pursuing Bush policies on Iran and Israel. As recently as yesterday, President Obama's Chairman of the US Joint Chiefs of Staff, Admiral Mike Mullen, responded when asked whether Iran was capable of building an atom bomb. Admiral Mullen replied, "We think they do, quite frankly."

So, it's clear. I'm about to step into marshy soil here, by noting that I found 19 questionable Obama policies or statements in his Joint Congressional speech delivered three days before his announcement that upon the end of the U.S. combat mission in Iraq, up to 50,000 U.S. troops could remain through 2011, after the "pullout".

And while various "mint" operations are peddling Obama "Change" coins for purchase, complete with a certificate of authenticity, I wade further into the muck by noting that the President continues the giveaway of our hard-earned coins to an economic team intent on keeping mismanagement structures in place, serving economic ends that do not constitute the common good. I would refer readers to the many statements that I issued during the final days of our Power to the People Green Party Presidential campaign about re-creating an economic system truly and finally owned by the people, operating in our interest. It is possible to do that. All it requires is enough political will.

But what forces me out into the open marshland of "non-mainstream" political punditry has to do with the latest Obama "pullout": the decision to withdraw from the April 2009 Geneva United Nations World Conference Against Racism, dubbed Durban II.

We heard the same palaver in 2001 from the same forces inside our country, basically that a discussion of Zionism, in the context of such a Conference, would be anti-Semitic; therefore all the world's dispossessed and marginalized people must continue to suffer and sacrifice while muting their grievances so that no discussion of Israel would take place on the world stage in this context....." (McKinney March 02 2009)

And we could go on. However I hope you get the gist. Anyway we will now go on to look at the Obama bailouts as he continues the process of turning private debt into public debt whilst the man and woman in the street slowly asphyxiate under a pillow of debt.

This is going to really hurt..most people - In getting to grips with understanding what Stephen Lendman, a Research Associate of the Centre for Research on Globalization, describes in his article, 'Obama's Latest No Banker Left Behind Scheme', as "..the greatest ever wealth transfer in the shortest span of time.."(Lendman 27 March 2009), one gets some idea of the enormous amounts of public money being transferred to private corporations and super rich individuals. In the aforementioned article Lendman sets out the scale of the public subsidies.

"Timothy Geithner unveiled his Public-Private Investment Program (PPIP) on March 23, the latest in a growing alphabet soup of handouts topping $12.5 trillion and counting - so much in so many forms... it's hard for experts to keep up let alone the public, except to sense something is very wrong. They're being fleeced by a finance Ponzi scheme, sheer flimflam, and here's how from what we know:

- $400 billion in taking over Fannie and Freddie;
- $42 billion for the auto giants; billions more coming for their suppliers;
- approaching $200 billion for AIG with more coming on request;

- $350 billion to Citigroup in handouts and loan guarantees;
- tens of billions to other banks, including $87 billion to JP Morgan Chase for bad Lehman Brothers trades;
- $700 billion for TARP I; half the money released under TARP II;
- over $200 billion and counting for the Term Asset-Backed Securities Loan Facility (TALF) to extend government-guaranteed loans for investors to buy "certain AAA-rated asset-backed securities (as a) component" of the Consumer and Business Lending Initiative (CBLI), established under the Emergency Economic Stabilization Act (EESA) of 2008;
- the $787 billion stimulus under the American Recovery and Relief Act of 2009 (ARRA);
- around $300 billion under the Homeowner Affordability and Stability Plan (HASP) - the so-called mortgage bailout plan;
- $50 billion backing for short-term corporate IOUs held by money market funds - from the Exchange Stabilization Fund (ESF), a vehicle established by a provision in the 1934 Gold Reserve Act for foreign exchange intervention to stabilize the value of the dollar;
- $500 billion for various credit market rescues;
- $620 billion for industrial nations' currency swaps;
- $120 billion for emerging economies' currency swaps;
- $1.25 trillion for Fannie and Freddie mortgage backed securities;
- $200 billion for Fannie, Freddie, and Federal Home Loan Bank bonds;
- way more than the announced $300 billion for longer-term Treasuries (mostly with 7 - 10 year maturities); the Fed's been buying billions of them since last year;
- Fed-expanded overnight lending to $2.4 trillion - free money at 0% interest;

- a reported $750 billion for banks in the FY 2010 budget - yet to be voted on and appropriated;
- a proposed $470 billion increase for the FDIC to borrow from the Treasury;
- perhaps hundreds of billions more in unannounced or hidden handouts in amounts and to whom the Fed and Treasury won't say; on March 14, AIG named its big counterparties for the first time with firms like Goldman Sachs, Societe Generale, Deutsche Bank, and Barclays showing up prominently; and now
- PPIP - the latest gift to Wall Street courtesy of taxpayers getting none of the gain and all the pain." (Lendman 27 March, 2009)

If your head is spinning, don't worry, it should be. The scale of the larceny is mindboggling whilst tens of millions of ordinary people in the US are generally left to drown in debt and the effects of long-term unemployment/under-employment.

Not surprisingly the stock market loved the increased flow of public funds into their collective coffers and the US stock market soared by around 7% on 23 March 2009 with banks and other financial institutions leading the way, no doubt salivating at the prospect of an unlimited supply of public alms for the super-rich. Basically, Geithner's *Toxic Asset Plan* involves subsidizing private investors to pay way over the odds for 'assets' that nobody wants with the guarantee that any losses will be picked up by the Federal Reserve, which in the end means taxpayers. It's a heads they win, tails we lose game for taxpayers.

Lendman tells us that, "Economist James Galbraith calls it another massive "ineffective" giveaway to banks with taxpayers getting hosed from a repackaged trash removal scheme that's been around since last fall when Geithner, as New York Fed president, planned it with Wall Street CEOs." (Lendman March 27 2009) I hope you have picked up on the revolving door between private Wall Street financial institutions and central government. Geithner is Wall Street's man doing Wall Street's bidding. He was hatching these giveaway schemes whilst in the 'private' sector and when he already no doubt had a strong inkling that he would either have a top post in the Obama administration – if Obama won the election; as looked likely – or be called upon as an advisor. We have foxes and wolves guarding the chicken coop.

Lendman really nails down the fundamental analytic failure which dooms Geithner's plans to failure. He cites economist James Galbraith who tells us:

"If Geithner's plan to fix the banks would also fix the economy," maybe the idea makes sense. "But no smart economist we know thinks that it will." It's a giant swindle, but that aside, Geithner has "five fundamental misconceptions:"

(1) *The trouble with the economy is that banks aren't lending, he says.*
In fact, it's because businesses and mainly households are way over-extended and "are now collapsing under the weight of it. As consumers retrench (of necessity), companies that sell to them (must also), thus exacerbating the problem. The banks, meanwhile, are lending," just not as much as they used to.
"Also, the shadow banking system (securitization markets), which actually provided more funding to the economy than the banks, has collapsed."

(2) *The banks aren't lending because their balance sheets are loaded with 'bad assets.'*
In fact, "banks aren't lending (enough) because they have decided to stop making loans to people and companies who can't pay them back" or don't want more loans in the first place. They're also scared that new debt will cause more write-offs, greater losses, and the threat they'll be wiped out entirely. So their strategy is hunker down and wait for a better time to do business.

(3) *Bad assets are "bad" because the market doesn't understand how much they're really worth.*
In fact, they're bad because "they are worth (lots) less than banks say they are." A major factor is the near-30%

drop in house prices wiping out over $5 trillion in valuations. Lenders want households to take losses because if they do it themselves they'll be wiped out. So PPIP arranges it for them.

(4) *Once "bad assets" are off balance sheets, banks will start lending again.*
In fact, banks will stay cautious until the housing market and economy improve. So far, that's nowhere in sight.

(5) *Once banks start lending, the economy will recover.*
In fact, house prices are falling, savings have been wiped out, huge job losses are continuing, and "consumers will have debt coming out of their ears" that will take years to work off.

Geithner's plan just shifts debt from lenders to taxpayers "where it will sit until the government finally admits that a major portion will never be paid back." Galbraith's conclusion: Geithner's plan is "extremely dangerous" besides being a scam to cheat the public. Why does Wall Street love it? Because it wrote it in the first place, so the whole scheme is arranged for its benefit - if it works.

It's a big "if" as investors want the lowest possible prices and banks the highest. The question is will they compromise and for what - the better quality junk investors want or the most toxic stuff banks want to offload for whatever they can get." (Lendman 27 March 2009)

In terms of solutions to begin to tackle the crisis in the banking sector, economist Nouriel Roubini, who actually predicted the current global economic crisis, suggests two courses of action, firstly; force banks to sell toxic assets at true value and take the losses; and secondly; shut down the insolvent ones, however it's unlikely you will see Geithner or Obama putting forward such sensible proposals. About the only thing that Obama's bailouts guarantee is that he will have to return to Congress in the not too distant future seeking more bailout money.

Obama and Brown paddling up the creek without a paddle – The Obama bank bailout is similar to that of Gordon Brown's UK government and both are destined for failure. Lendman cites an article by Dan Roberts in the London Guardian On March 24 headlined: "US follows UK – on the wrong road." In this article Roberts suggests that "Geithner's plan "aims to achieve roughly the same as the British government's (bad loans) insurance for the Royal Bank of Scotland and Lloyds. So how do the two schemes compare?"

Details aside, they "work on the same principle: that banks will (behave) normally again and (benefit) the economy (once) they're protected from past mistakes. But these responses underestimate the scale of the crisis." Geithner's plan covers not just toxic assets but many ordinary bank loans as well.

"Similarly, the assets put forward by Lloyds in the UK insurance scheme include every buy-to-let mortgage issued by HBOS, not just the ones already in default. Judge the banks on their actions (not just their words), and you would conclude this crisis has some way to go. Yet both governments assume banks (suffer) from a crisis of confidence (simply cured) by removing (toxic debt) uncertainty. What neither seems willing to acknowledge is the likelihood that much of their lending has gone for good; that this is not a liquidity crisis, but a solvency (one)." Britain's plan didn't work and neither will Washington's." (Lendman citing Roberts March 27 2009)

Obama may be able to survive the electoral consequences of his administration's terrible blunders given that the crisis came to fruition under a Republican administration, however Brown looks doomed to electoral failure and for being most noteworthy as a Prime Minister who never won an election.

Once again we will draw on the work of Paul Craig Roberts and Michael Hudson who whilst representing somewhat differing political and economic perspectives agree on the ill conceived and futile nature of the Obama bailouts as well as the fact that President Obama is a representative of the ruling oligarchy.

Obama, bought and sold, like those who preceded him – In an article entitled *'President Of Special Interests'* Paul Craig Roberts tells us that:

"The Bush/Obama bailout/stimulus plans are not going to work. Both are schemes hatched by a clique of financial insiders. The schemes will redistribute income and wealth from American taxpayers to the shyster banksters, who have destroyed American jobs, ruined the retirement plans of tens of millions of Americans, and worsened the situation of millions of people worldwide who naively trusted American financial institutions. The ongoing theft has simply been recast. Instead of using fraudulent financial instruments, the banksters are using government policy.

Michael Hudson captures the nature of the heist in *CounterPunch* (February 12, 2009):

"When it comes to cleaning up the Greenspan Bubble legacy by writing down homeowner mortgage debt, the Treasury proposal offers homeowners $50 billion – just [half of one percent] of the $10 trillion Wall Street bailout to date, and less than half the amount given to AIG to pay its hedge fund speculators on their derivative gambles. The Treasury has handed out $25 billion to each and every big bank, so just two of these banks alone got as much as the reported one-quarter of all homeowners in America suffering from Negative Equity on their homes and in need of mortgage renegotiation. Yet today's economic shrinkage cannot be reversed without a recovery in consumer demand. The economy has lost the "virtual wealth" in higher-priced homes and the stock market, and must rely on after-tax earnings. But I see little concern for wage earners in the Treasury plan. Without debt relief, consumer spending and business investment will not recover."

Roberts tells us, "The big money men cannot conceive of anyone's suffering except the mega-rich. If billions are not at stake, what is the problem? How can a family losing its house bring down the economy?"

There was a time in America when the interests of elites were connected to those of ordinary Americans. Henry Ford said that he paid his workers good wages so they could buy his cars.

Today American corporations pay foreign workers low wages so CEOs can pay themselves multi-million dollar "performance" bonuses.

The American economic elite are hiding their treason to the American people behind "free trade".

I want to say this as clearly as it can be said. The offshoring of American jobs is the antithesis of free trade. Free trade is based on comparative advantage. Jobs offshoring is an activity in pursuit of lowest factor cost – an activity that David Ricardo, the originator of the free trade theory, described as the betrayal of one's own country in pursuit of "absolute advantage".

The "free market" shills on the payroll of the U.S. Chamber, NAM, and in economics departments and think tanks that are recipients of grants from transnational corporations are whores aligned with elites who are destroying the American work force.

Obama has appointed to his National Economic Council blatant apologists for the offshoring of American jobs.

Possibly Obama loves the country that elevated him to its highest office. But his administration is populated with people whose loyalty does not extend beyond elites to the American people." (Roberts 19 February 2009)

It's the Debts stupid - We now move on to Michael Hudson's analysis of Obama's economic recovery plans. Hudson has repeatedly warned against the dangers of trying to solve the problem of an economic crisis resulting from the bursting of an asset price bubble built on huge debt by creating a new asset price bubble based upon even greater debt.

In his article entitled **'Finance Capitalism Hits a Wall, The Oligarchs' Escape Plan – at the Treasury's Expense** *www.globalresearch.ca* Professor Michael Hudson starts out by reminding us that the money as debt scam has had a good run for our money.

"The financial "wealth creation" game is over. Economies emerged from World War II relatively free of debt, but the 60-year global run-up has run its course. Finance capitalism is in a state of collapse, and marginal palliatives cannot revive it. The U.S. economy

cannot "inflate its way out of debt," because this would collapse the dollar and end its dreams of global empire by forcing foreign countries to go their own way. There is too little manufacturing to make the economy more "competitive," given its high housing costs, transportation, debt and tax overhead. A quarter to a third of U.S. real estate has fallen into Negative Equity, so no banks will lend to them. The economy has hit a debt wall and is falling into Negative Equity, where it may remain for as far as the eye can see until there is a debt write-down."

In terms of the failure of elected representatives, political officials and advisors to act effectively in the face of this crisis he reiterates the points I made earlier about the *placemen* and women who occupy these positions and act at the behest of Wall Street.

"There is no sign that Mr. Obama's economic advisors, Treasury officials and heads of the relevant Congressional committees recognize the need for a write-down. After all, they have been placed in their positions precisely because they do not understand that debt leveraging is a form of economic overhead, not real "wealth creation". But their tunnel vision is what makes them "reliable" to Wall Street, which doesn't like surprises. And the entire character of today's financial crisis continues to be labelled "surprising" and "unexpected" by the press as each new surprisingly pessimistic statistic hits the news. It's safe to be surprised; suspicious to have expected bad news and being a "premature doomsayer". One must have faith in the system above all. And the system was the Greenspan Bubble. That is why "Ayn Rand Alan" was put in charge in the first place, after all."

Hudson goes on to reinforce how the years of 'boom' were built upon a mirage where assets would continue to grow in value without any connection to the real economy in what was in effect a debt based Ponzi scheme.

"So the government tries to recover the happy Bubble Economy years by getting debt growing again, hoping to re-inflate real estate and stock market prices. That was, after all, the Golden Age of finance capital's world of using debt leverage to bid up the book-price of fictitious capital assets. Everyone loved it as long as it lasted.

Voters thought they had a chance to become millionaires, and approved happily. And at least it made Wall Street richer than ever before – while almost doubling the share of wealth held by the wealthiest 1% of America's families. For Washington policy makers, they are synonymous with "the economy" – at least the economy for which national economic policy is being formulated these days.

The Obama-Geithner plan to restart the Bubble Economy's debt growth so as to inflate asset prices by enough to pay off the debt overhang out of new "capital gains" cannot possibly work. But that is the only trick these ponies know. We have entered an era of asset-price deflation, not inflation. Economic data charts throughout the world have hit a wall and every trend has been plunging vertically downward since last autumn. U.S. consumer prices experienced their fastest plunge since the Great Depression of the 1930s, along with consumer "confidence," international shipping, real estate and stock market prices, oil and the exchange rate for British sterling. The global economy is falling into depression, and cannot recover until debts are written down."

So whilst Hudson suggests that writing down debts, amongst other things, is critical to kickstarting a US and global economic recovery he notes how this does not even appear to be on the radar of the Obama administration.

"Instead of doing this, the government is doing just the opposite. It is proposing to take bad debts onto the public-sector balance sheet, printing new Treasury bonds, give the banks bonds whose interest charges will have to be paid by taxing labor and industry.

As in Third World austerity programs, the effect of keeping the debts in place at the "real" economy's expense will be to shrink the domestic U.S. market – while providing opportunities for hedge funds to pick up depreciated assets cheaply as the federal government, states and cities sell them off. This is called letting the banks "earn their way out of debt". It's strangling the "real" economy, because not a dollar of the government's response has been devoted to reducing the overall debt volume."

He goes on to highlight the relatively tiny amount of money the 'Pope of Hope' is devoting to assisting ordinary working people in the

US who are struggling in the face of falling property prices, job losses and overwhelming debt.

"Take the much-vaunted $50 billion program designed to renegotiate mortgages downward for "troubled homeowners". Upon closer examination it turns out that the real beneficiaries are the giant leading banks such as Citibank and Bank of America that have made the bad loans. The Treasury will take on the bad debt that banks are stuck with, and will permit mortgagees to renegotiate their monthly payment down to 38% of their income. But rather than the banks taking the loss as they should do for over-lending, the Treasury itself will make up the difference – and pay it to the banks so that they will be able to get what they hoped to get. The hapless mortgage-burdened family stuck in their negative-equity home turns out to be merely a passive vehicle for the Treasury to pass debt relief on to the commercial banks.

Few news stories have made this clear, but the *Financial Times* spelled out the details buried in small print. It added that the Treasury has not yet decided whether to write down the debt principal for the estimated 15 million families with negative equity (and perhaps 30 million by this time next year as property prices continue to plunge). No doubt a similar deal will be made: For every $100,000 of write-down in debt owed by over-mortgaged homeowners, the bank will receive $100,000 from the Treasury. Government debt will rise by $100,000, and the process will continue until the Treasury has transferred $50,000,000,000 to the banks that made the reckless loans.

There is enough for just 500,000 of these renegotiations of $100,000 each. Hardly enough to make much of a dent, but the principle has been put in place for many further bailouts." (Hudson 17 February 2009)

So we see that even the relative crumbs that the Obama administration offers the vast majority of the US public is simply another way transferring public funds to private corporations.

At this point I need to interject quotes from another of Michael Hudson's articles, which focuses upon the media storm surrounding bonuses for senior managers. This article highlights the calculated deceit of President Obama and other leading politicians with their mock outrage and crocodile tears over greed in Wall Street whilst off camera they feed the financial monster live babies. Hudson puts the AIG bonuses furore in perspective by highlighting that,

"It may seem odd, but the public outrage against $135 million in AIG bonuses is a godsend to Wall Street, AID scoundrels included. How can the media be so preoccupied with the discovery that there is self-serving greed to be found in the financial sector? Every TV channel and every newspaper in the country, from right to left, have made these bonuses the lead story over the past two days.

Here's the problem with all the hoopla over the $135 million in AIG bonuses: This sum is only less than 0.1% – one thousandth – of the $183 BILLION that the U.S. Treasury gave to AIG as a "pass-through" to its counterparties. This sum, over a thousand times the magnitude of the bonuses on which public attention is conveniently being focused by Wall Street promoters, did not stay with AIG. For over six months, the public media and Congressmen have been trying to find out just where this money DID go. Bloomberg brought a lawsuit to find out. Only to be met with a wall of silence.

Until finally, on Sunday night, March 15, the government finally released the details. They were indeed highly embarrassing. The largest recipient turned out to be just what earlier financial reporters had said was rumored: Mr. Paulson's own firm, Goldman Sachs, headed the list. It was owed $13 billion in counterparty claims. So here's the picture that's emerging. Last September, Treasury Secretary Paulson, from Goldman Sachs, drew up a terse 3-page memo outlining his bailout proposal. The plan specified that whatever he and other Treasury officials did (thus including his subordinates, also from Goldman Sachs), could not be challenged legally or undone, much less prosecuted. This condition enraged Congress, which rejected the bailout in its first incarnation.

It now looks as if Mr. Paulson had good reason to put in a fatal legal clause blocking any clawback of funds given by the Treasury to AIG's counterparties. This is where public outrage should be focused.

Instead, the leading Congressional shepherds of the bailout legislation – along with Mr. Obama, who came out in his final, Friday night presidential debate with Sen. McCain strongly in favor of the bailout in Mr. Paulson's awful "short" version – have been posing as conspicuously as possible for the media to cover a deflected target – the AIG executives receiving bonuses, not the company's counterparties.

There are two questions that one always must ask when a political operation is being launched. First, qui bono? Who benefits? And second, why now? In my experience, timing almost always is the key to figuring out the dynamics at work.

Regarding qui bono, what does Sen. Schumer, Rep. Frank, Pres. Obama and other Wall Street sponsors gain from this public outcry? For starters, it depicts them as hard taskmasters of the banking and financial sector, not its lobbyists carrying water for one giveaway after another. So the AIG kafuffle has muddied the water about where their political loyalties really lie. It enables them to strike a misleading pose – and hence to pose as "honest brokers" next time they dishonestly give away the next few trillion dollars to their major sponsors and campaign contributors.

Regarding the timing, I think I have answered that above. Talking about AIG bonuses has effectively distracted attention from the AIG counterparties who received the $183 billion in Treasury giveaways. The "final" sum to be given to its counterparties has been rumored to be $250 billion, so Sen. Schumer, Rep. Frank and Pres. Obama still have a lot more work to do for Wall Street in the coming year or so.

To succeed in this work – while mitigating the public outrage already rising against the bad bailouts – they need to strike precisely the pose that they're striking now. It is an exercise in deception.

The moral should be: The wetter the crocodile tears shed over giving bonuses to AIG individuals (who seem to be largely on the healthy, bona fide insurance side of AIG's business, not its hedge-fund Ponzi-scheme racket), the more they will distract public attention from the $180 billion giveaway, and the better they can position themselves to give away yet more government money (Treasury bonds and Federal Reserve deposits) to their favorite financial charities." (Hudson 18 March 2009)

These are the issues Obamaites should be discussing. They need to move beyond his smooth rhetoric, easy charm and faux emotions and start to recognise that unless they are believers in Manifest Destiny, the CNN version of US history or in the top 1% of earners they have been had, big time.

Returning to Professor Hudson's earlier article on the Oligarchs' Escape Plan he sets out how the neo-liberal corporatist version of the history of European economic theory was in fact based upon a deliberate rewriting of the theories of the founding fathers of European economic theory. They turned that which was traditionally seen as economically extractive i.e. rent and interest into productive phenomena and gave free rein to private banks to invent money as debt and hold the real economy hostage. He concludes that:

"Today it is easier to see that the Western economies cannot go on the way they have been. They have reached the point where the debts exceed the ability to pay. Instead of recognizing this fact and scaling debts back into line with the ability to pay, the Obama-Geithner plan is to bail out the big banks and hedge funds, keeping the volume of debt in place and indeed, growing once again through the "magic of compound interest". The result can only be an increasingly extractive economy, until households, real estate and industrial companies, states and cities, and the national government itself is driven into debt peonage.

The alternative is a century and a half old, and emerged out of the ideals of the classical economic doctrines of Adam Smith, David Ricardo, John Stuart Mill, and the last great classical economist, Marx. Their common denominator was to view rent and interest as extractive, not productive. Classical political economy and its successor Progressive Era socialism sought to nationalize the land (or at least to fully tax its rent as the fiscal base). Governments were to create their own credit, not leave this function to wealthy elites via a bank monopoly on credit creation. So today's neoliberalism paints a false picture of what the classical economists envisioned as free markets. They were markets free of economic rent and interest (and taxes to support an aristocracy or oligarchy). Socialism was to free economies from these overhead charges. Today's Obama-Geithner rescue plan is just the reverse." (Hudson 17 February 2009)

Conclusion

In reading this chapter I am hopeful that the following points will be as apparent to you as they are to me:

- Subprime mortgages were not the principle cause of the financial crisis. If they had been why did the rescue package not address the problem of bad mortgage debt directly by refinancing troubled mortgages and paying off foreclosed mortgages rather than giving public money to banks?
- Excess debt and financial deregulation are at the heart of this crisis.
- The whole issue of subprime mortgages became a convenient excuse to blame poor US citizens (disproportionately made up of Afrikans and other non-Caucasians) for a problem engineered by predominantly rich Caucasian males. It was also used to gloss over the longstanding, systematic and ongoing discrimination in the provision of mortgages and other financial services to Afrikan people in the US.
- Economic boom and bust is inherent in a system founded upon ever increasing levels of personal and institutional debt and unrestrained greed and wild financial gambling.
- The initial financial bailout package put together in the US under the Bush administration, although appearing large paled into insignificance when compared to the sort of money doled out by the US Federal Reserve in soft loans to banks in the days whilst they were apparently waiting for the initial bailout package to be approved by the legislators. It is also comparatively small when compared to the money that cannot be accounted for in the US defence department's annual accounts, and tiny when compare to the incredible amount of money wagered on derivatives. The cumulative total of all the myriad bailouts is however huge at over $12 trillion and counting.

- These types of periodic economic collapses simply concentrate additional wealth in the hands of a very small segment of the population and involve the transfer of assets from the poor to the rich. If there are winners and losers and the winners are in a position to precipitate such a collapse is it really beyond the realms of possibility that these are not the freakish accidental series of chain reactions as depicted by the corporate media? Remember JP Morgan published rumours that a prominent bank in New York faced insolvency which led to a spiral of bankruptcy and insolvency in 1907. This led to a congressional investigation led by Nelson Aldrich, who later married into the Rockerfeller family and who was deeply connected to the banking cartels. The commission recommended the setting up of a central bank so that such a financial crisis would never take place again. In 1913 President Woodrow Wilson enacted the legislation (the Federal Reserve act was written by bankers) that created the US Federal Reserve and the rest is history.
- The Federal Reserve and other central banks are at the heart of these financial crises and are not the solutions. Each of these crashes is preceded by huge increases in the money supply followed by a sudden curtailment of lines of credit. Check out the US crash of 1929.
- Corruption is at the heart of corporate capitalism despite what you might be led to believe. One of the ways in which the US government (under Bush junior) was able to push through its much touted initial bailout package was by the addition of $150 billion of bribes described as 'earmarks'. These bribes are standard procedure when enacting legislation in the US and are divided 60:40 between the ruling majority and minority parties. The monies are then spent on pet projects in the legislators' home states.
- The US government, Republican and Democrat, have been deliberately manipulating government economic

statistics to present a picture of the economy that is far removed from reality. This manipulation is important in preventing the type of public unrest that would result if people became fully aware that inflation is far outstripping their wage rises and unemployment is millions higher than officially reported. US workers are working longer hours to compensate for the decreasing buying power of their devalued dollars.

- The Obama administration represents business as usual. Obama and his colleagues in government are servants of the Wall Street financiers and their policies and priorities reflect this.
- The money invested in bailing out the man and woman in the street is tiny compared to the trillions that are being served up to bolster financial corporations and are little more than a sop to the corporate media watching (and believing) masses.

The US led economic system is built on sand, however it will remain intact so long as the dollar remains the currency in which oil is bought and sold and so long as it remains the world's reserve currency. Despite the weakness of the US economy the dollar rose dramatically towards the end of 2008, as spooked investors ran to the world's reserve currency for cover. However don't be fooled by short term spikes, during the next 2-4 years we are going to see a huge crash in the value of the dollar when the Chinese, Japanese and sovereign wealth funds eventually refuse to bankroll the US' addiction to debt.

THE GREAT DEPRESSION?

Could the 2008 economic crisis develop into the type of depression experienced by the USA and other parts of the world between 1929 and the late 1930s, or the sort of crisis experienced in Russia in the 1990s? And if this were to happen how would the growing crisis unfold?

Dmitry Orlov, a Russian engineer and writer who specialises in predicting economic collapses, gave a presentation at the Community Solutions Conference in Michigan in November 2008, entitled 'The Five Stages Of Collapse'. This talk was reproduced as an article on 13 November, 2008 on the www.countercurrents.org website. In his talk Orlov presented his ideas for how he believes the US economy will (continue to) collapse. The table below provides a summary of the key elements of Orlov's five stages of collapse.

As suggested in the chart on the next page Orlov believes this process of collapse in the US is well underway. In January 2008 he published an article on *"The Five Stages of Collapse,"* in which he defined the five stages, and then stated that the US was in the midst of a financial collapse. Whilst suggesting that different people will experience the five stages at different times and in different ways he suggests that the US faces the prospect of entering the stage of commercial collapse. He states that "Stages 2 and 3 - commercial and political collapse, are driven by financial collapse, and will overlap each other. Right now, it is unclear which one is farther along. On the one hand, there are signs that global shipping is grinding to a halt, and that big box retailers are in for a very bad time, with many stores likely to close following a disastrous Christmas season. On the other hand, states are already experiencing massive budget shortfalls, laying off state workers, cutting back on programs, and are starting to beg the federal government for bail-out money." (Orlov 13 Nov 2008)

In the UK one has seen the collapse of the 100 year old Woolworths retail chain in late November 2008 as well as the MFI DIY chain going into administration at the same time. These retail sector casualties promise to be but the first victims of this recession.

Orlov has come to some of his conclusions by comparing the US economy with what happened to the Russian economy in the 1990s.

Stage of Collapse	Description of Stage	Before	After	The Remedy
1: Financial Collapse	Faith in 'business as usual' is lost. The future can no longer be assumed to resemble the past. Risk can no longer be assessed and financial assets guaranteed.	• Retirement Savings • Home equity • Investments • Cash savings • Credit transactions • Financial independence	• Govt aid • Charity • Squatting • Pennies on the dollar • Hyperinflation • Cash/barter transactions • Physical interdependence	Live without needing (much) money
2. Commercial Collapse	Faith that 'the market shall provide' is lost. Commodities are hoarded. Import and retail chains break down. Widespread shortages of survival necessities become the norm	• Money is scarce • Service economy • All you can eat • Shopping malls • Supermarkets • Cult of the new • Imported products	• Products are scarce • Self-service economy • All you can scrounge • Flea Markets • Farm stands • Keeping it running • Domestic substitutes	Provide for basic needs
3. Political Collapse	It is sometimes hard to discern political collapse, because politicians tend to be quite good at maintaining the pretence of power and authority even as it dwindles. But there are some telltale signs of political collapse. One is when politicians start moonlighting because their day job is no longer sufficiently gainful. Another is when regional politicians start to openly defy orders from the political center. Russia experienced plenty of each of these symptoms.	• Entitlements • Municipal services • Taxes and budgets • Police protection • Trash removal • Roads and bridges	• Broken promises • Municipal favors • Graft, 'freelancing' • Military patrols • Neighbourhood trash heaps • Potholes and detours	Local self-government
4. Social Collapse	Faith that 'your people will take care of you' is lost. Local social institutions, be they charities or other groups that rush in to fill the power vacuum, run out of resources or fail through internal conflict	• Solidarity • Mutual aid • Neighbourhood groups • Diversity	• Every man for himself • Confrontation • Roaming gangs • Ethnic cleansing	Cohesive community, mutual responsibility
5. Cultural Collapse	Faith in the goodness of humanity is lost. People lose their capacity for 'kindness, generosity, consideration, affection, honesty, hospitality, compassion, charity'	• We can recognize ourselves and each other	• We can no longer recognize ourselves or each other	Classical human virtues

In making this comparison he pays particular attention to what he terms 'energy flows' believing that the US economy is highly vulnerable to large fluctuations in the price of oil as the Russian economy was in the late 1980s although for different reasons. He tells us that:

"What happened in the late 80s is that Russian oil production hit an all-time peak. This coincided with new oil provinces coming on stream in the West - the North Sea in the UK and Norway, and Prudhoe Bay in Alaska - and this suddenly made oil very cheap on the world markets. Soviet revenues plummeted, but their appetite for imported goods remained unchanged, and so they sank deeper and deeper into debt. What doomed them in the end was not even so much the level of debt, but their inability to take on further debt even faster. Once international lenders balked at making further loans, it was game over.

What is happening to the United States now is broadly similar, with certain polarities reversed. The US is an oil importer, burning up 25% of the world's production, and importing over two-thirds of that. Back in mid-90s, when I first started trying to guess the timing of the US collapse, the arrival of the global peak in oil production was scheduled for around the turn of the century. It turned out that the estimate was off by almost a decade, but that is actually fairly accurate as far as such big predictions go. So here it is the high price of oil that is putting the brakes on further debt expansion. As higher oil prices trigger a recession, the economy starts shrinking, and a shrinking economy cannot sustain an ever-expanding level of debt. At some point the ability to finance oil imports will be lost, and that will be the tipping point, after which nothing will ever be the same."

So, he suggests that whilst the Russians suffered because of a collapsing oil price so the US will suffer because of an increasing oil price. Whilst there is some validity in this hypothesis there are some critical differences between the Soviet and US situation. Firstly, the US has a far more broad based economy than the Soviet Union did and has the capacity to innovate quickly and already has the technological capacity to reduce its dependency on oil if the political will is present. Secondly, it was not the burgeoning oil price – which reduced dramatically again in the second half of 2008 – which precipitated the collapse in financial markets and ensuing recession (I will show in a later chapter that the US has really been in recession since 2001). Thirdly, there is plenty of debate and controversy over the 'peak oil' date i.e. the date at which world oil production peaks and starts to fall. At present it looks as if this time could be several decades away. Finally, it is rare that a multifaceted problem can be adequately explained in relation to one single factor such as an increase in the price of oil.

Orlov correctly identifies the US economy's unsustainable level of indebtedness as the critical problem and highlights how this could be addressed in a way which would cause huge pain around the world.

"It is instructive to ask the question, Who are we borrowing this bail-out money from? People will tell you that we are borrowing it from "the taxpayer... Who is "the taxpayer" going to borrow this money from in the meantime? From other Americans? No, because our savings rate has been abysmally low for quite some time now, and what little we have saved is in housing equity, which is dwindling, and in stocks and bonds, through mutual funds and 401ks and such, which are down by a third or so. The value of these investments is crashing, and if we dumped these investments to raise the cash to fund this new debt, that would just make them crash even faster. In effect, we'd only be moving money from one pocket to another. So, really, the bailouts have to be financed by foreigners. And what if these foreigners decide not to trust us with any more of their savings? Then our only recourse is to "monetize" the debt: to print money.

And so the next question is, how much money would we have to print? The purpose of the bailouts is to provide liquidity to insolvent companies, to avoid deleveraging. To understand what that means, we have to understand that for every actual dollar within the economy, in the sense of it not being borrowed, there are over 13 dollars of borrowed money, which only exists while the debt can be rolled over. If our credit is maxed out while the economy is growing, that's bad enough, but the US economy is shrinking because of the recent oil shock. A smaller economy cannot carry as much debt, and this is part of the reason why we have deleveraging. Once the process of debt going sour gets started, it is hard to stop, and if deleveraging were to run its course, we would be down over 1300%. To monetize that much debt would require over 1300% inflation. And once that gets started, it becomes very hard to stop.

And, that, believe it or not, is actually the good news. Because most of our debt is denominated in our own currency – the US dollar – the US will not have to declare sovereign default, like Russia was forced to do in the 1990s. Instead, we can inflate our way out of national bankruptcy, by printing a lot of dollars. We will repay our national debt, but we will do so in worthless paper money, bankrupting our international creditors in the process. There is sure to be plenty of pain for everyone, especially everyone who is used to having plenty of money, because their money will no longer make the world go around. Once the US has to start earning foreign currency in order to pay for imports, you can be sure that imports will become quite scarce."

The latter inflationary 'get out of debtors jail card' for the US economy is highly unlikely, however already China and Russia have been talking about reducing their dependency on the US dollar and trading between each other in different currencies. The world is becoming increasingly nervous about bankrolling the US addiction to debt and there is likely to be a spectacular collapse in the value of the US dollar before the end of 2010. At the very least one result of the current economic turmoil is that the dollar will lose its singular place as the world's reserve currency.

I think it unlikely that the US economy will implode to the same degree as happened in Russia in the1990s, however this recession promises to be deep and protracted and nothing like the usual 18 month contractions that have characterised US recessions since the mid 1850s.

Hold onto your hats, it's going to get rougher still.

Economic Boom and Bust – As inevitable as Sunrise and Sunset?

Introduction

I am sure you have heard politicians, economists, newsreaders and others talking about the need to break out of a cycle of economic boom and bust. Indeed the present UK Prime Minister, Gordon Brown and the previous UK Prime Minister, Tony Blair, used to singularly and jointly boast as to how they had broken the UK's boom and bust cycle! As my Mother used to tell me 'self-praise is no recommendation' and 'pride before a fall'. Of course, Blair is well out of it, now earning around £10 million a year on the lecture circuit, endowed by the corporate interests he used to serve as UK Prime Minister. Gordon Brown is left to clean up the mess, which unlike Barack Obama – who will have plenty of mess to shovel –he helped to create.

The aim of this chapter is to demonstrate that in an economy built upon an ever expanding mountain of debt and where saving is unfashionable and unrestrained reckless gambling on the financial markets is encouraged, cycles of economic boom and bust are as inevitable as sunrise and sunset.

There follows a series of diagrams which pictorially depict the economic cycle of boom and bust. Hopefully one or all of these diagrams will reinforce the point that; based upon the existing economic order, in which manipulation by powerful vested interests is standard practice; cycles of boom and bust are inevitable and inherent in the operation of almost all economies around the world.

The following diagram depicts the economic cycle as a graph. We shall now describe each of the phases depicted in the graph.

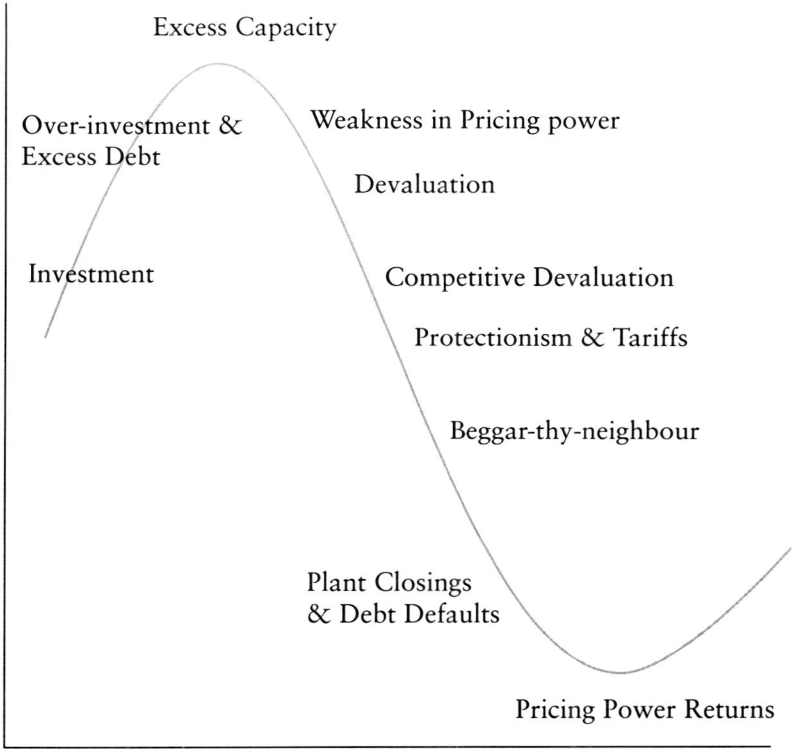

Source: *http://www.nowandfutures.com/forecast.html*

Investment phase

The diagram begins with a period of growing investment. During this phase house prices are rising rapidly, interest rates are low and either stable or falling steadily, the (official) inflation rate is low and stable, share prices are rising rapidly and (official) unemployment is low and stable or falling slowly. Levels of personal indebtedness increase significantly as credit is made available on easy terms and many people remortgage to take advantage of the rapid rise in house prices.

Over investment and excess debt

Most people have short economic memories and get caught up in the feel good feeling of an economic boom. In this phase households become overextended with personal debt, banks and other financial institutions engage in ever more risky investments and expand their debt:asset ratios to dangerous levels. The government, instead of saving for a rainy day continues to spend as if high growth levels will continue forever. People view their homes as an investment rather than a place to live and many get locked into the buy-to-let market which expands rapidly.

Excess capacity

Too much housing, too much stocks of products coupled with weakening demand as consumer spending falls as interest rates begin to rise and people realise they are overextended, means there is excess capacity in relation to demand.

Weakness in pricing power

The investopedia website tells us that pricing power is:

"An economic term referring to the effect that a **change** in a firm's product price has on the quantity demanded of that product. Pricing power ties in with the "Price Elasticity of Demand".

They go on to say that,

"Generally speaking, if a company doesn't have much pricing power then an increase in their prices would lessen the demand for their products."

Source: *http://www.investopedia.com/terms/p/pricingpower.asp?viewed=1*

What the foregoing means is that demand in the economy is weakening. When demand is strong companies generally have strong pricing power and can increase their prices without too much of a negative effect on demand. The weakness in pricing power is linked to the weakness in demand and the weakness in demand is linked to the excess of debt in the economy.

Devaluation

As the economy weakens and growth slows, interest rates are cut to try to stimulate consumer demand and in particular the moribund housing market. A significant fall in interest rates leads to a sharp fall in the value of the currency. As the interest rate falls and the currency is devalued; foreign investors and governments are less inclined to finance the government's debt by buying their Treasury Bonds. These interlocking circumstances lead to credit rating agencies marking down the country's credit rating (there was talk in late 2008 of the US losing its AAA credit risk rating and similar talk in the UK in May 2009).

Competitive Devaluation

As the economic crisis grows some countries may take steps to devalue their currency (particularly by reducing interest rates). "There are two implications for a currency devaluation. First, devaluation makes a country's exports relatively less expensive for foreigners and second, it makes foreign products relatively more expensive for domestic consumers, discouraging imports. As a result, this may help to reduce a country's trade deficit." *http://www.investopedia.com/terms/d/devaluation.asp*

The downside is that a rapidly falling currency weakens the government's as well as consumer spending power which can be very important, particularly for poorer countries which rely on importing manufactured products from richer countries. Attacks from currency speculators also exacerbate the devaluation which can run out of control.

Protectionism and Tariffs

Protectionism occurs when a country introduces trade barriers i.e. legal or administrative measures to prevent or make more difficult the import of foreign products. These measures may include the attachment of tariffs, which are in effect taxes, to the import of certain products from all or particular countries. A country may also introduce a cap or limit on the volume or number of a particular product that can be imported from overseas. Now, one should be clear that countries generally believe in free trade when it is to their economic advantage. For example the powerful European Union, which claims to be a champion of free trade, entered into negotiations with China to limit the import of Chinese textiles into the EU. With

Chinese manufacturers able to massively undercut the prices of European manufacturers, a free trade in textiles would have led to the decimation of textile manufacturing in Western Europe. On the other hand rich countries such as the US provide massive subsidies to domestic farmers producing cotton, rice and other products which are then used to flood and take over markets in poorer countries.

Beggar-thy-Neighbour

In this phase, which is probably where the UK is at the time of writing (December 2008), things get very rough and more and more people turn to, family, friends and charity to help them through tough times as their access to credit runs out. An example of how bad things had got in the US in late 2008 was highlighted by an article entitled 'Down On The Farm, A Frenzy Over Free Food' by Allison Sherry that appeared in the Denver Post. Perry's article described the events that took place when the Miller family, who own a 600 acre farm outside of Platteville, about 37 miles north of Denver invited people to come to the farm to gather surplus produce. Sherry reports that:

"Want one more palpable sign of a desperate economy? An estimated 40,000 people came to a Weld County farm Saturday to collect free potatoes, carrots and leeks. Cars snaked around cornfields and parallel parked along Colorado 66 and 119 early in the morning to get free food from the Miller family…

As this prolonged Indian summer continued, the Millers had decided to give away produce because so much was left over at the end of their annual fall festival. Any day now, a few deep freezes would kill it off.

They expected between 5,000 and 10,000 people spread out over a couple of days. Instead, they found themselves on Saturday morning inundated with cars and people with sacks and wagons and barrels ready to harvest whatever was available.

The Millers cancelled the second day of the giveaway originally planned for today because, as Chris Miller put it, "the pickins' are very slim now."

At one point, 30 acres of family farmland had become a parking lot. Their crowd estimate of 40,000 plus was based on the number of cars. Sheriff's officials said they "wouldn't be surprised" if that count was accurate...

"Overwhelmed is putting it mildly," Miller said. "People obviously need food."

Evidently, Platteville isn't the only place where this is the case. Last week in Denver, thieves broke into freezers owned by the Park Hill Grandparents Organization and stole Thanksgiving trimmings – including more than a dozen frozen turkeys – set to be donated.

And in Lakewood on Saturday, people lined up in the dark at 6 a.m. to collect Thanksgiving boxes, donated by the Jeffco Action Center. By the end of the day, 5,141 people had gotten food – the biggest demand in 40 years."

'Down On The Farm, A Frenzy Over Free Food', By Allison Sherry November 24, 2008 *The Denver Post,* reproduced in *www.informationclearinghouse.com*

This article highlights the huge underbelly of poverty amongst both the unemployed as well as the working poor in 'the most powerful nation on Earth'. However the huge number of working poor in the US is not surprising when one considers that the minimum wage in the US is only $6.55 up from $5.85 on 24 July 2008. It should also be remembered that the federal minimum wage was $5.15 for a decade until 2007 "when legislation mandated three increases over three years. In 2009, the minimum wage will rise again to $7.25. In calculating the yearly earnings of a minimum-wage earner at the current rate, it comes out to about $13,100/year (before taxes). That hardly seems like a reasonable income, even if you're living in a very low cost-of-living area." *http://blogs.payscale.com/salary_report_kris_cowan/2008/08/what-is-the-min.html*

Plant closings and debt defaults

Obviously each of these phases of the cycle are not discrete and one need only watch, read or listen to the news to realise that this phase is well entrenched around the world. From the USA to China and the UK large factories are closing on a weekly or even daily basis. The crisis in the financial markets preceded and precipitated the crisis in the 'real economy' and now all the dominos are falling..quickly. The difficulty in getting access to credit, which was deliberately precipitated by the Federal Reserve in the US, compounds the difficulties faced by companies and households. Unemployment continues to rise dramatically; houses are repossessed in large numbers as prices fall by between 20-40% from their peak levels.

Pricing Power returns

Things start to get better before people start to feel better off, just as things get worse before people start to feel worse off. The recovery lag is probably 6-12 months and during this period people have reordered their personal finances, companies that have weathered the storm have worked hard to improve their competitiveness, government has started to reduce the budget deficit and interest rates have stabilised and the currency begins to recover. Companies which had, earlier in the cycle, cut prices to the bone, sometimes selling products at cost to maintain turnover and market share in a deflationary spiral, are now able to cautiously increase prices. The bottom has been hit and the slow process of recovery starts the cycle all over again.

The Emotional Ups and Downs of the Economic Cycle?

We will now move on to look at another representation of the foregoing economic cycle which focuses on people's emotional response to the prevailing macro-economic conditions.

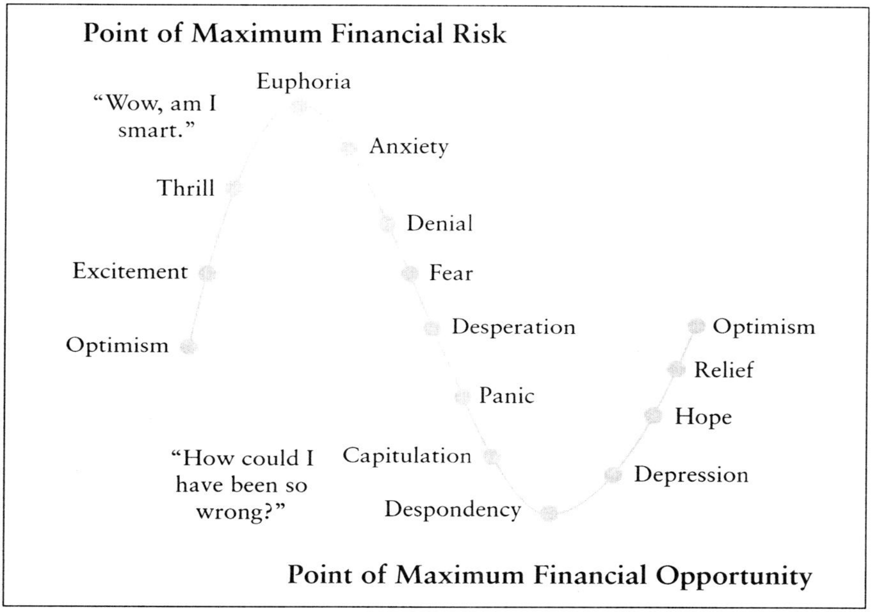

Source: *http://www.nowandfutures.com/images/RiskVsOpportunity. jpg*

The above graph describes the emotional rollercoaster which can be correlated with the previous description of macro-economic conditions throughout an economic cycle. Whilst the diagram does not require a great deal of analysis the most striking feature of the graph is that the emotions are probably two to three stages out of synch with what people should be feeling if they interpreted the macroeconomic signals more rationally. For example, at the Point of Depression people should be experiencing renewed Optimism as the economy begins experiencing an upturn. Similarly, at the point of euphoria, those who have overextended themselves should be experiencing anxiety at the thought that strong growth cannot continue forever and at signs of an overheating economy. Of course there are a smaller number of huge winner during the bad times. These are the elites who engineer recessions and depressions, such as JD Rockerfeller who made an estimated $200,000,000 ($1.9,000,000,000 in today's money) during the Great Depression of the late 1920s and 1930s), as well as those who have kept their personal debt low and have access to capital with which to buy up devalued assets.

There is a saying that investment is about time and not timing, which highlights that the vast majority of people, be they the man or woman on the street, or high powered investment managers cannot accurately predict the beginning or end of a boom or recession. Therefore if you can hold onto your investments for long enough without too much discomfort you will generally come out with a profit.

The Market Cycle

Our final diagram below provides a circular model to relate the macro-economic cycle to the (stock) market cycle.

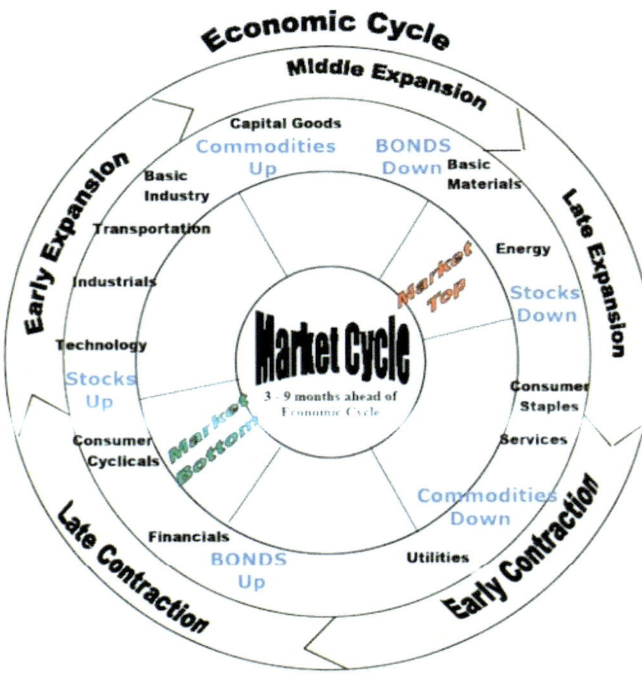

Source: *http://www.nowandfutures.com/images/economic_cycle (matt_blackman).jpg*

As you can see Matt Blackman's diagram suggests that the market cycle operates between 3-9 months ahead of the economic cycle. I.e. the stock market peaks 3-9 months before growth in the wider economy peaks and similarly bottoms out 3-9 months before the economy ceases to contract. One can compare this diagram to the previous two diagrams and see the clear correlations. At the time of writing this text (December 2008) the UK economy was in the 'Early Contraction' phase of the economic cycle having experienced (officially) one quarter of negative economic growth and seemingly about to record a second successive quarter of negative growth when the figures for quarter three (Oct-Dec) were released in January 2009. In the UK the widely accepted definition of recession is two successive quarters of negative growth.

As you can see in the Early Contraction phase Commodity prices fall and there was a tremendous fall in oil prices in the second half of 2008 as demand fell dramatically in line with a contraction in the world economy. Of course not only oil, but other commodities fall in price as well in this phase and this has a severe impact on the economies of already impoverished countries – particularly in Afrika – which often rely upon selling one or two commodities as their primary source of foreign exchange. With these countries being so poor they cannot even adopt the OPEC strategy of reducing supply in order to shore up the price of their respective commodities.

In the middle of the early contraction phase shares in utility companies increase strongly as interest rates are cut as government attempts to stimulate the economy.

Utilities are "A category of stocks for utilities such as gas and power. The utilities sector contains companies such as electric, gas and *water* firms and integrated providers.

Because utilities require significant infrastructure, these firms often carry large amounts of debt. With a high debt load, utilities companies become sensitive to changes in the interest rate. As *interest rates* rise or drop, the debt payments will increase or decrease. The utilities sector performs best when interest rates are falling or remain low. *http://www.investopedia.com/terms/u/utilities_sector.asp*

In the Late Contraction phase Bonds go up, particularly

government issued bonds which are seen as a safe haven for investors, as in general countries cannot go bankrupt. A bond is:

"simply an 'IOU' in which an investor agrees to loan money to a company or government in exchange for a predetermined interest rate." *http://beginnersinvest.about.com/cs/bondbasics/f/whatisabond.htm*

In the late contraction phase of the economic cycle interest rates are at or near their lowest point in the cycle and as investors anticipate the bottoming out of share prices the financials sector begins to look more attractive.

Financials are "A category of stocks containing firms that provide financial services to commercial and retail customers. This sector includes banks, investment *funds*, insurance companies and real estate.

Financial services perform best in low interest rate environments. A large portion of this sector generates revenue from mortgages and loans, which gain value as interest rates drop. Furthermore, when the *business* cycle is in an upswing, the financial sector benefits from additional investments. Improved economic conditions usually lead to more capital projects and increased personal investing. New projects require financing, which usually leads to a larger number of loans." *http://www.investopedia.com/terms/f/financial_sector.asp*

After the market has bottomed out and shares prices slowly begin to rise investors begin to invest in the consumer cyclical sector as the recession nears its end. Consumer cyclicals are:

"A category of stocks that rely heavily on the business cycle and economic conditions. **Consumer cyclicals** include industries such as *automotive*, housing, entertainment and retail. The category can be further divided into durable and non-durable sections. Durable cyclicals include physical goods such as hardware or vehicles, while non-durables represent items like movies or hotel services.

The performance of consumer cyclicals is highly related to the state of the economy. They represent goods and services that are not considered necessities, but luxurious purchases. During contractions or recessions, people have less disposable *income* to spend on consumer cyclicals. When the economy is expanding or booming, the sales of these goods rises as retail and leisure spending increase."

http://www.investopedia.com/terms/c/consumer_cyclicals.asp

As mentioned earlier the market bottoms out before the end of the economic contraction and when the economy does enter the Early Expansion phase the stocks that are in strong demand relate to the building blocks of the economy i.e. technology, industrials, transportation and basic industry. In the Middle expansion phase Commodity prices begin to rise sharply again as the prices of capital goods and stocks in companies involved in this area rise.

Capital goods include factories, machinery, tools, equipment, and various buildings which are used to produce other products for consumption. Capital goods, then, are products which are not produced for immediate consumption; rather, they are objects that are used to produce other goods and services. These types of goods are important economic factors because they are key to developing a positive return from manufacturing other products and commodities. *http://en.wikipedia.org/wiki/Capital_goods*

At the end of the middle expansion phase the return on bonds goes down as government and other bond issuers have had their coffers swelled by a period of sustained economic growth/profitability and hence do not have such an urgent need to borrow from financial markets and hence offer lower rates of interest on any bonds they do issue.

Prices of stocks in basic materials also rise sharply at this phase in the economic cycle. **Basic materials** are:

"A category of stocks that accounts for companies involved with the discovery, development and processing of raw materials. The basic materials sector includes the mining and refining of metals, chemical producers and forestry products.

The basic materials sector is sensitive to changes in the *business* cycle. Because the sector supplies materials for construction, it depends on a strong economy. This sector is also sensitive to supply and demand fluctuations because the price of raw materials, such as gold or other metals, is largely demand driven." *http://www.investopedia.com/terms/b/basic_materials.asp?viewed=1*

In the early part of the late expansion phase of the economic cycle the major indices of stock prices such as the FTSE 100 or Dow Jones Index peak whilst shares in companies in the energy sector are riding high as demand for energy surges with a booming economy.

The **Energy sector** comprises "A category of stocks that relate to producing or supplying energy. This sector includes companies involved in the exploration and development of oil or *gas reserves*, oil and gas drilling, or integrated power firms.

Performance in the sector is largely driven by the supply and demand for worldwide *energy*. Energy producers will do very well during times of high oil and gas prices, but will earn less when the value of energy drops. Furthermore, this sector is sensitive to political events, which historically have driven changes in the price of oil." *http://www.investopedia.com/terms/e/energy_sector.asp*

Share prices begin to decline slowly in the second half of the late expansion phase and the stocks of companies involved in producing consumer staples are in demand. **Consumer staples** relate to "The industries that manufacture and sell food/beverages, tobacco, prescription drugs and household products." *http://www.investopedia.com/terms/c/consumerstaples.asp*

As the economy enters the early contraction phase investors gravitate towards companies involved in the services sector. The **Services sector** produces what are sometimes referred to as intangible goods and involves industries such as insurance, government, tourism banking, education, waste disposal, business services, and real estate. Etc.

And so the cycle repeats itself, as inevitably as sunrise and sunset (with similar variations in time periods) with a little help from the economic elite who engineer boom and bust and reap the rewards of each.

LIES, DAMNED LIES AND GOVERNMENT STATISTICS

The title of this chapter is a reworking of a well known saying which encapsulates the cynicism most people feel about statistics produced by governments. In this chapter I will demonstrate how well founded this cynicism is and that in this instance the general public's common sense view represents good sense.

The hidden numbers

Let's look at some additional information that has generally failed to break through the informational stranglehold of the corporate media.

Former US Secretary of State for Defense, Donald Rumsfeld, admitted under questioning by Congresswoman Cynthia McKinney, whilst appearing before a congressional committee, that he could not explain why the Pentagon was unable to account for $2,300,000,000,000 ($ 2.3 trillion) of expenditure from its 1999 accounts and $1,100,000,000,000 from its 2000 accounts. Rumsfeld admitted that the Pentagon was "unable to track these transactions". When one thinks about these figures and compares them to the $700billion bailout of financial institutions - which was beefed up to over $800 billion after the addition of financial goodies to appease members of congress – one can see that there is a much larger picture that is not being presented to the vast majority of the public. Furthermore it was reported by John Parry and Jamie McGeever (Reuters New York/London) that whilst the Federal Reserve was waiting for the bailout package to be approved by the US legislature it was providing on average $188 billion per day in 'sweetheart loans' to financial institutions. This manifested as $1,570,000,000,000 of loans between 21st September 2008 to 29 September 2008. To reinforce this point, on 29 September Bloomberg news agency reported that the Federal Reserve pumped $630 billion into financial markets on the day after the bailout was first rejected. *http://www.corbettreport.com*

The trouble with writing a book like this in the midst of economic chaos is that as fast as one attempts to quantify how high the dung is piled up, another trailer load is dumped on the pile. Therefore the figures cited need to viewed like photographs, as capturing a particular moment in time. However the following figures give you an idea of how the bailout dung heap was measuring up in December 2008.

In an article entitled 'Excess Debt And Deflation = Depression', Stephen Lendman cites the work of Jim Bianco to provide a comparative and absolute measure of the scale of the 2008 bailout in the US. As you will see it is absolutely breathtaking.

"An unprecedented-sized bailout assures greater trouble ahead. Using inflation-adjusted numbers, Jim Bianco of Bianco Research said that bailout-related debt cost more than the following combined:

- the Marshall Plan - cost: $12.7 billion; inflation-adjusted cost: $115.3 billion;
- the Louisiana Purchase - cost: $15 million; inflation-adjusted cost: $217 million;
- NASA's Apollo human spaceflight program - cost: $36.4 billion; inflation-adjusted cost: $237 billion;
- the S & L crisis - cost: $153 billion; inflation-adjusted cost: $256 billion;
- the Korean War - cost: $54 billion; inflation-adjusted cost: $454 billion;
- the New Deal - cost: an estimated $32 billion; inflation-adjusted cost: an estimated $500 billion;
- the invasion and early months of the Iraq War (not the total war cost to date that's far higher) - cost: $551 billion; inflation-adjusted cost: $597 billion;
- the Vietnam War - cost: $111 billion; inflation-adjusted cost: $698 billion; and
- NASA since inception - cost: $416.7 billion; inflation-adjusted cost: $851.2 billion.

Total: $3.92 trillion compared to around $8.5 trillion in bailout funds allocated or pledged thus far with these numbers certain to go higher." (Stephen Lendman15 December, 2008 Countercurrents.org)

When one considers that the total size of the US economy is around $13 trillion dollars this is a recipe for disaster and that clucking you can hear is the sound of debt collecting chickens coming home to roost.

Hidden Inflation

Now where is all this money coming from? As noted in an earlier chapter this money is debt money created by financial institutions. Now, even an A Level/High school economics student knows that if you increase the money supply without a commensurate increase in economic production this should lead to an increase in inflation since you have more money chasing the same amount of goods. However we have seen massive increases in the money supply, but we have not seen a commensurate huge increase in inflation in the US and other 'western economies'. This gives credence to the calculation by John Williams as cited earlier by Paul Craig Roberts above that the US inflation rate reached 13.2 percent in 2008. The first table below shows the trend in the official US inflation rate from January 1980 up until July 2008. As you can see the long term trend line in red is just above 5% in 1990 and finishes just above 5% in July 2008. This is a fraud being perpetrated on the unwitting public to hide the decline in their real earnings and spending power. To highlight this point BBC News in covering the 2008 US elections in October 2008 reported that the real earnings of the average US citizen was the same as it had been in 1979. This despite all the hype about decades of continuous economic growth in 'the west'.

Walter J. "John" Williams was born in 1949. He received an A.B. in Economics, cum laude, from Dartmouth College in 1971, and was awarded an M.B.A. from Dartmouth's Amos Tuck School of Business Administration in 1972, where he was named an Edward Tuck Scholar. During his career as a consulting economist, he has worked with individuals as well as Fortune 500 companies.

In the table below, taken from his *www.shadowstats.com* website he compares the official government consumer price index (CPI) inflation figures between 1980 and 2008 with the CPI over that period if the US government had maintained the same counting methodologies used in 1980.

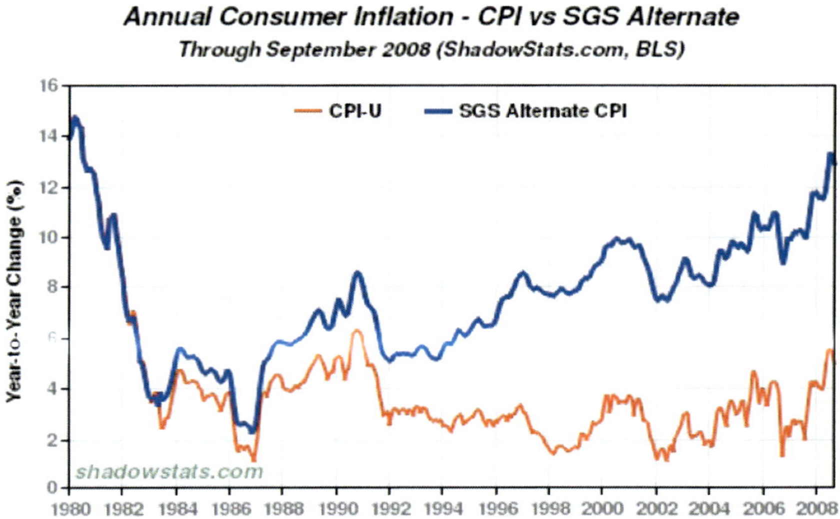

The CPI on the Alternate Data Series tab here, reflects the CPI as if it were calculated using the methodologies in place in 1980.

Williams provides an excellent analysis of how inflation has come to be so dramatically underestimated in government statistics in the US – much of this also applies to the UK as well.

"Inflation, as reported by the Consumer Price Index (CPI) is understated by roughly 7% per year. This is due to recent redefinitions of the series as well as to flawed methodologies, particularly adjustments to price measures for quality changes.

The CPI was designed to help businesses, individuals and the government adjust their financial planning and considerations for the impact of inflation. The CPI worked reasonably well for those purposes into the early-1980s. In recent decades, however, the reporting system increasingly succumbed to pressures from miscreant politicians, who were and are intent upon stealing income from social security recipients, without ever taking the issue of reduced entitlement payments before the public or Congress for approval.

In particular, changes made in CPI methodology during the Clinton Administration understated inflation significantly, and, through a cumulative effect with earlier changes that began in the late-Carter and early Reagan Administrations have reduced current social security payments by roughly half from where they would have been otherwise. That means Social Security checks today would be about double had the various changes not been made. In like manner, anyone involved in commerce, who relies on receiving payments adjusted for the CPI, has been similarly damaged. On the other side, if you are making payments based on the CPI (i.e., the federal government), you are making out like a bandit.

In the original version of this background article, I noted that Social Security payments should be 43% higher, but that was back in September 2004 and only adjusted for CPI changes that took place after 1993. The current estimate adjusts for methodology gimmicks introduced since 1980.

Let Them Eat Hamburger

In the early 1990s, press reports began surfacing as to how the CPI really was significantly overstating inflation. If only the CPI inflation rate could be reduced, it was argued, then entitlements, such as social security, would not increase as much each year, and that would help to bring the budget deficit under control. Behind this movement were financial luminaries Michael Boskin, then chief economist to the first Bush Administration, and Alan Greenspan, Chairman of the Board of Governors of the Federal Reserve System.

Although the ensuing political furor killed consideration of Congressionally mandated changes in the CPI, the BLS quietly stepped forward and began changing the system, anyway, early in the Clinton Administration.

Up until the Boskin/Greenspan agendum surfaced, the CPI was measured using the costs of a fixed basket of goods, a fairly simple and straightforward concept. The identical basket of goods would be priced at prevailing market costs for each period, and the period-to-period change in the cost of that market basket represented the rate of inflation in terms of maintaining a constant standard of living.

The Boskin/Greenspan argument was that when steak got too expensive, the consumer would substitute hamburger for the steak, and that the inflation measure should reflect the costs tied to buying hamburger versus steak, instead of steak versus steak. Of course, replacing hamburger for steak in the calculations would reduce the inflation rate, but it represented the rate of inflation in terms of maintaining a declining standard of living. Cost of living was being replaced by the cost of survival. The old system told you how much you had to increase your income in order to keep buying steak. The new system promised you hamburger, and then dog food, perhaps, after that.

The Boskin/Greenspan concept violated the intent and common usage of the inflation index. The CPI was considered sacrosanct within the Department of Labor, given the number of contractual relationships that were anchored to it. The CPI was one number that never was to be revised, given its widespread usage.

Shortly after Clinton took control of the White House, however, attitudes changed. The BLS initially did not institute a new CPI measurement using a variable-basket of goods that allowed substitution of hamburger for steak, but rather tried to approximate the effect by changing the weighting of goods in the CPI fixed basket. Over a period of several years, straight arithmetic weighting of the CPI components was shifted to a geometric weighting. The Boskin/Greenspan benefit of a geometric weighting was that it automatically gave a lower weighting to CPI components that were rising in price, and a higher weighting to those items dropping in price.

Once the system had been shifted fully to geometric weighting, the net effect was to reduce reported CPI on an annual, or year-over-year basis, by 2.7% from what it would have been based on the traditional weighting methodology. The results have been dramatic. The compounding effect since the early-1990s has reduced annual cost of living adjustments in social security by more than a third.

Changes estimated by the BLS show roughly a 4% understatement in current annual CPI inflation versus what would have been reported using the original methodology. Adding the roughly 3% lost to geometric weighting – most of which was not included in the BLS estimates – takes the current total CPI understatement to roughly 7%.

Traditional inflation rates can be estimated by adding 7.0% to the CPI-U annual growth rate (3.8% +7.0% = 10.8% as of August 2006) or by adding 7.4% to the C-CPI-U rate (3.4% + 7.4% = 10.8% as of August 2006).

Hedonic Thrills of Using Federally Mandated Gasoline Additives

Aside from the changed weighting, the average person also tends to sense higher inflation than is reported by the BLS, because of hedonics, as in hedonism. Hedonics adjusts the prices of goods for the increased pleasure the consumer derives from them. That new washing machine you bought did not cost you 20% more than it would have cost you last year, because you got an offsetting 20% increase in the pleasure you derive from pushing its new electronic control buttons instead of turning that old noisy dial, according to the BLS.

When gasoline rises 10 cents per gallon because of a federally mandated gasoline additive, the increased gasoline cost does not contribute to inflation. Instead, the 10 cents is eliminated from the CPI because of the offsetting hedonic thrills the consumer gets from breathing cleaner air. The same principle applies to federally mandated safety features in automobiles. I have not attempted to quantify the effects of questionable quality adjustments to the CPI, but they are substantial.

Then there is "intervention analysis" in the seasonal adjustment process, when a commodity, like gasoline, goes through violent price swings. Intervention analysis is done to tone down the volatility. As a result, somehow, rising gasoline prices never seem to get fully reflected in the CPI, but the declining prices sure do.

How Can So Many Financial Pundits Live Without Consuming Food and Energy?

The Pollyannas on Wall Street like to play games with the CPI, too. The concept of looking at the "core" rate of inflation-net of food and energy-was developed as a way of removing short-term (as in a month or two) volatility from inflation when energy and/or food prices turned volatile. Since food and energy account for about 23% of consumer spending (as weighted in the CPI), however, related inflation cannot be ignored for long. Nonetheless, it is common to hear financial pundits cite annual "core" inflation as a way of showing how contained inflation is. Such comments are moronic and such commentators are due the appropriate respect.

Too-Low Inflation Reporting Yields Too-High GDP Growth

As is discussed in the final instalment on GDP, part of the problem with GDP reporting is the way inflation is handled. Although the CPI is not used in the GDP calculation, there are relationships with the price deflators used in converting GDP data and growth to inflation-adjusted numbers. The more inflation is understated, the higher the inflation-adjusted rate of GDP growth that gets reported.

Source: *The Consumer Price Index* (Part Four in a Series of Five) October 1, 2006 Update (September 22, 2004 Original) *http://www.shadowstats.com/article/56*

Before moving on to demonstrate the huge increase in the money supply in the US economy it is worth recalling the $1,000,000,000,000,000 liabilities held in derivatives whilst remembering that it has been calculated that the total value of all the assets on Earth is only $100,000,000,000,000 i.e. ten times less than the value of derivatives. This really is economic madness.

It's the money supply stupid

What is this thing they call money supply.

"In *economics*, **money supply**, or **money stock**, is the total amount of money available in an *economy* at a particular point in time.[1] There are several ways to define "money", but each includes *currency* in circulation and *demand deposits*. [2][3]" http://en.wikipedia.org/wiki/Money_supply

The table below shows the huge growth in the United States money supply between 1960 and 2005.

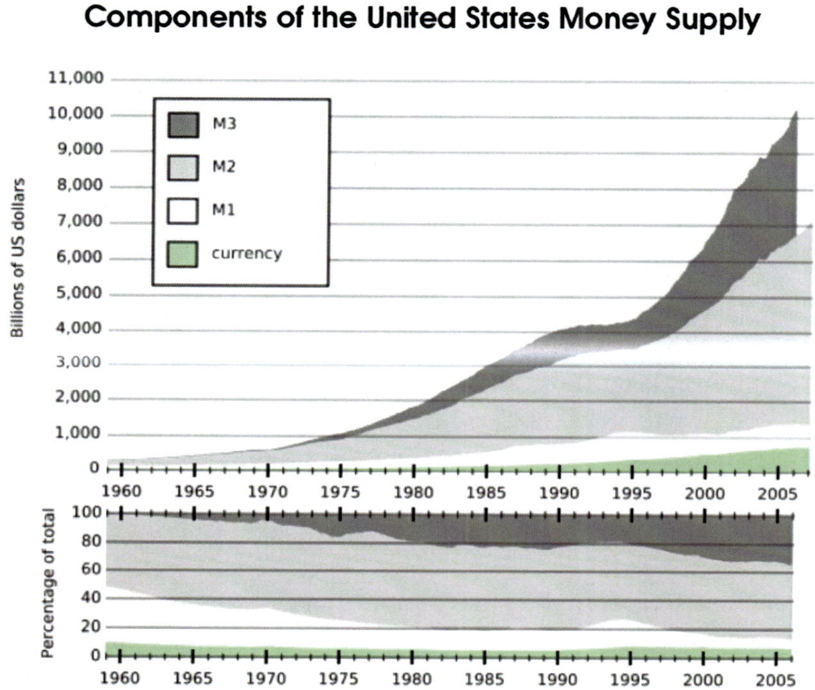

Source: http://en.wikipedia.org/wiki/Image:Components_of_the_United_States_money_supply2.svg

The wikipedia website source (which is referenced) provides the following definitions of the components of the money supply.

- **M0**: Physical *currency*. A measure of the money supply which combines any liquid or cash assets held within a central bank and the amount of physical currency circulating in the economy. M0 is the most liquid measure of the money supply. It only includes cash or assets that could quickly be converted into currency.[7]
- **M1**: Physical currency circulating in the economy + demand deposits (i.e. checking account deposits). This is a measure used by economists trying to quantify the amount of money in circulation. M1 is a very liquid

measure of the money supply, as it only contains cash and assets that can also be used for payments.[8]

- **M2**: M1 + *time deposits*, savings deposits, and non-institutional money-market funds. M2 is a broader classification of money than M1. Economists also use M2 when looking to quantify the amount of money in circulation and trying to explain different economic monetary conditions. [9] M2 is a key economic indicator used to forecast inflation.[10]
- **M3**: M2 + large time deposits, institutional money-market funds, short-term repurchase agreements, along with other larger liquid assets. This is the broadest measure of money commonly used and is used by economists to estimate the entire supply of money within an economy.[11]"

As you will notice from the money supply chart M3 and M2 represent a rapidly growing proportion of the money supply, increasing from just over 50% of total money supply in 1960 to over 85% in 2005.

Fractional-reserve banking

The different forms of money in government money supply statistics arise from the practice of fractional reserve banking which was described earlier in this book. Whenever a bank gives out a loan in a fractional-reserve banking system, a new type of debt money is created.

"This new type of money is what makes up the non-**M0** components in the **M1-M3** statistics. In short, there are two types of money in a fractional-reserve banking system[12][13]:

1. **central bank money** (physical currency)
2. **commercial bank money** (money created through loans) - sometimes referred to as **checkbook money**[14]

In the money supply statistics, **central bank money** is **M0** while the **commercial bank money** is divided up into the **M1-M3** components.

Generally, the types of commercial bank money that tend to be valued at lower amounts are classified in the narrow category of **M1** while the types of commercial bank money that tend to exist in larger amounts are categorized in **M2** and **M3**, with **M3** having the largest.

The Federal Reserve ceased publishing M3 statistics in March 2006. They explained that M3 did not convey any additional information about economic activity compared to M2, and thus, had not been used in determining monetary policy for years. Therefore, the costs to collect M3 data outweighed the benefits the data provided.[16] Some politicians have spoken out against the Federal Reserve's decision to cease publishing M3 statistics and have urged the U.S. Congress to take steps requiring the Federal Reserve to do so. Congressman *Ron Paul* claimed that "M3 is the best description of how quickly the Fed is creating new money and credit. Common sense tells us that a government central bank creating new money out of thin air depreciates the value of each dollar in circulation.[17]"

http://en.wikipedia.org/wiki/Money_supply

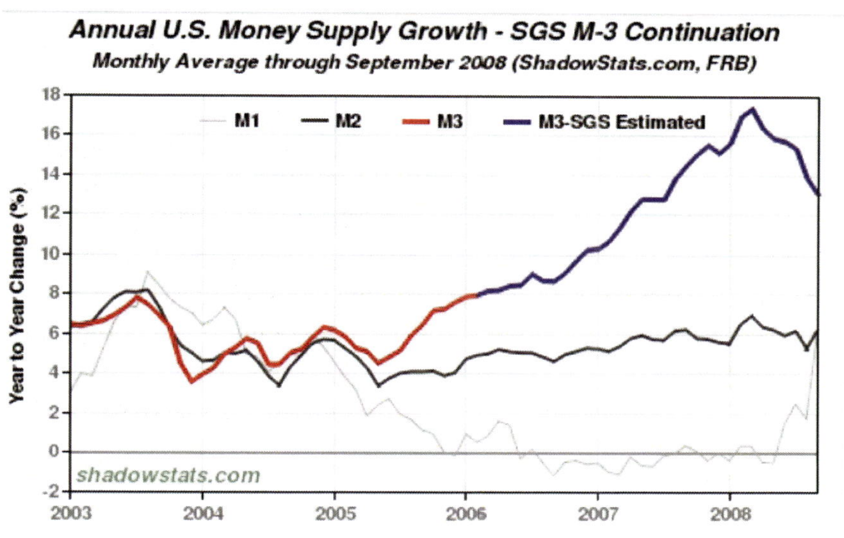

As mentioned earlier increasing the money supply should lead to an increase in inflation, and increases in inflation often lead to a decrease in GDP, hence why the Federal Reserve does not want US legislators or the public to know how much money they are creating and introducing into the economy. With all of the bailouts and financial rescue packages in 2008 one can only imagine what the M3 statistics for 2008 would be if the Fed would publish them. Well we are now going to look in further detail at the link between money supply and inflation.

Monetary exchange equation

"Money supply is important because it is linked to *inflation* by the "monetary exchange equation":

$$MV = PQ$$

M is the total dollars in the nation's money supply
V is the number of times per year each dollar is spent
P is the average price of all the goods and services sold during the year
Q is the quantity of goods and services sold during the year...

In other words, if the money supply grows faster than real GDP growth (described as "unproductive debt expansion"), inflation is likely to follow ("inflation is always and everywhere a monetary phenomenon"). *http://en.wikipedia.org/wiki/Money_supply*

The increase in the US money supply and decrease in the real spending power of the US dollar have gone hand in hand. In 2007 one would have needed $21.60 dollars to match the spending power of $1 in 1913 when the Federal Reserve was created. This is a devaluation in the dollar's spending power of 96%. (*www.Zeitgeistfilms.com*)

U.S. M3 money supply as a proportion of gross domestic product.

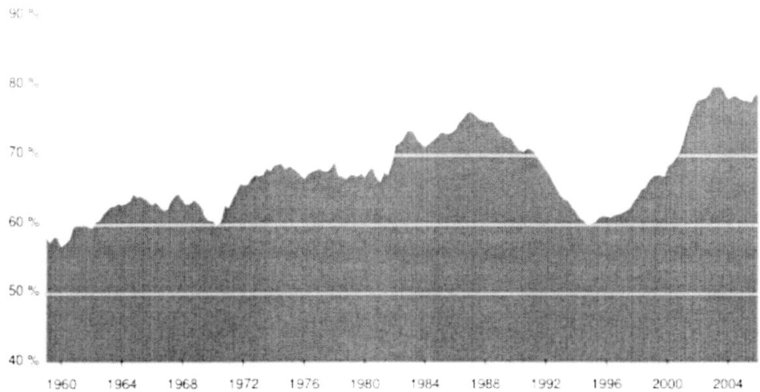

Source:*http://en.wikipedia.org/wiki/Image:Us_proportionate_m3.svg*

The chart above indicates the huge growth in money supply as a proportion of GDP from below 60% in 1960 and peaking at just over 80% in around 2003. The only thing that can follow such growth is a significant growth in inflation and depreciation in the real value of your money.

GDP – When growth is contracting

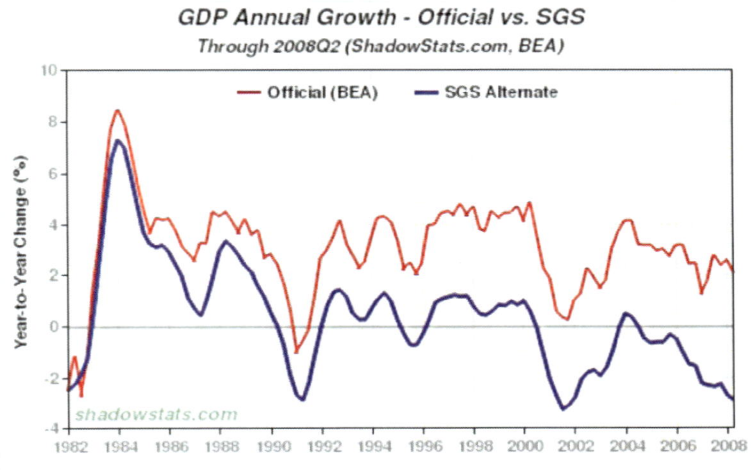

We have seen what government has managed to do to keep the official inflation statistics as low as possible, so now let's look at how they reverse the magic and keep the GDP figures as high possible, turning deep recession into simply slowing growth and low growth into economic boom. Once again this is an area where the average citizen's experiential analysis, or gut instinct (as with inflation), probably gives a better guide as to the state of the economy than the massaged and manipulated government statistics. In October 2008 it was reported that the UK economy had contracted by 0.5% for the quarter July-September 2008. This was supposed to have been the first such quarterly fall in UK GDP since 1992 when Britain was supposed to have entered a golden age of continued economic growth. Since an economic recession is technically two successive quarters of negative growth, the UK was simply experiencing a downturn as of October 2008, albeit with recession appearing inevitable, which turned out to be the case when the GDP figures showed a further contraction for the October-December 2008 quarter.

In this section, once again utilising the work of John Williams, you will see how GDP measures are inflated to keep the general public duped. I am concentrating on the US simply because it is the world's largest economy, the dollar is the world's reserve currency and the US has been the epicentre of the global financial crisis. If we can understand what has happened there we can understand what has happened in other places around the world. The GDP measure and other statistics we are covering in this chapter are like an economic placebo convincing the patient they are getting better as disease ravages their body. Williams tells us that:

"The Gross Domestic Product (GDP) is one of the broader measures of economic activity and is the most widely followed business indicator reported by the U.S. government. Upward growth biases built into GDP modeling since the early 1980s, however, have rendered this important series nearly worthless as an indicator of economic activity. The analysis in this Instalment will indicate that the recessions of 1990/1991 and 2001 were much longer and deeper than currently reported, and that lesser downturns in 1986 and 1995 were missed completely in the formal GDP reporting process. Furthermore, the current economic circumstance is suggestive of an early-1980s-style double-dip recession.

The distortions from bad GDP reporting have major impact within the financial system. For example, Alan Greenspan's heavy reliance on productivity gains to justify some of his policies is equally flawed, since the methods applied to GDP estimation influence the numerator in the productivity ratio. As with the CPI distortions discussed in Instalment III, the Federal Reserve Chairman knows better.

With reported growth moving up and away from economic reality, the primary significance of GDP reporting now is as a political propaganda tool and as a cheerleading prop for Pollyannaish analysts on Wall Street.

Deflation Wonders

As emphasized earlier, the lower the inflation rate that is used to deflate the GDP, the higher will be the resulting inflation-adjusted growth.

One of the deflation stars is the computer. While computer prices have come down over time, the quadrupling and re-quadrupling of memories provided with a standard computer have, through hedonics and quality adjustments (see Installment III on the CPI), enhanced the decline in prices used in deflating computer consumption in the GDP. According BEA deflators, $1,000 computers bought in 1990, 1995 and 2000 would cost $48.63, $95.84 and $526.58, respectively, today. I bought computers in each of those time frames and could not replicate any one of them for the suggested proportionate price in deflated dollars, regardless of free memory enhancement.

A Tempting Target for Manipulation

In the introduction to this series on government reporting, I mentioned political manipulation of the GNP/GDP in the Johnson and first Bush administrations that went beyond overly positive methodological changes. In both instances, my sources were consulting clients who had been involved directly in the process. In the latter instance, an individual at the BEA also confirmed the situation.

Few people argue with the GNP/GDP reports, so when Lyndon Johnson kept sending the initial GNP estimates back to the Commerce Department for correction, he eventually got what he wanted, and the media dutifully reported stronger than actual economic growth.

Near the end of the first Bush administration, an outside-the-system manipulation was worked. A senior member of the Executive Branch approached a senior officer of a large computer company and requested that reporting of computer sales to the BEA be inflated. This was done specifically to help with the reelection effort. The request was granted, and thanks to the heavy leverage of computer deflation, reported GDP growth enjoyed an artificial spike.

There are suggestions of other direct manipulations over time, specifically involving the Clinton administration and the current Bush administration. Most recently, a bizarre annual revision to the GDP data eliminated the 2001 recession, at least as traditionally defined with two consecutive quarters of real GDP contractions

Estimating Economic Reality

Based on my analysis of the GDP/GNP revisions and redefinitions over time, over-deflation and economic reporting as published before later political corrections, reporting of real GDP growth at present is overstated by roughly three percent per year against a more realistic, pre-Pollyanna Creep period.

Where the period of bloated GDP reporting began after the severe double-dip recession of 1980 and 1981/1982, it includes the last two recessions that were severe enough to generate reported GDP contractions. Both the 1990/1991 and 2001 recessions were deeper and longer than currently estimated. The recession from July 1990 to March 1991 (timing per the NBER) really began in late-1989 and persisted into 1992, perhaps even 1993. Such was evident in the underlying data of the time. Due to the NBER's early call of the recession's end, however, the first "jobless recovery" was seen.

Similarly, the recession that was timed from March to November 2001, began in late-2000 and persisted into 2003. Again, because of an early call to the recession's end, a "jobless recovery" was seen.

There also were economic downturns in 1986 and 1995 that were evident to most companies dealing in real world economic activity at the time. Although the contractions showed up in a number of measures, they were not severe enough to turn bloated GDP growth negative.

As the economy once again appears to be faltering, or losing traction, risk is high of renewed or a double-dip recession, of which the 2001 downturn eventually will be counted as the first leg.

I have only touched upon some of the highlights in problems with GDP reporting. Unfortunately, though widely followed, the series is probably the least meaningful of the major economic statistics followed by investors and the financial media."

Source: *"GOVERNMENT ECONOMIC REPORTS: THINGS YOU'VE SUSPECTED BUT WERE AFRAID TO ASK!"* A Series Authored by Walter J. "John" Williams "Gross Domestic Product" (Part Five in a Series of Five) October 6, 2004 *http://www.shadowstats.com/article/57*

No Jobs for the Boys or Girls

OK, it has been heavy going in this chapter, but we are almost there. The final area or statistical chicanery in the US economy that we are going to look at is in the measuring of unemployment.

The table below indicates the wide disparity in the measure of unemployment when one compares the official (U3) figures, the Bureau of Labor Statistics (U6) measure and Shadow Government Statistics estimates based upon earlier government methodologies that have now been abandoned.

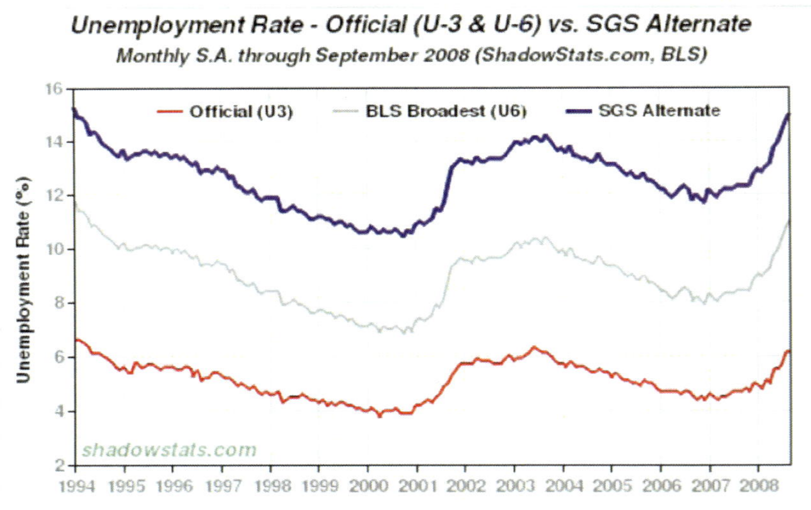

The SGS Alternate Unemployment Rate reflects current unemployment reporting methodology adjusted for SGS-estimated "discouraged workers" defined away during the Clinton Administration added to the existing BLS estimates of level U-6 unemployment.

In reviewing the government unemployment data Williams tells us that:

"The Bureau of Labor Statistics (BLS), U.S. Department of Labor, conducts two monthly surveys of U.S. employment and unemployment. Results usually are released on the first Friday of the month following the survey:

Household Survey (also **Current Population Survey**) – The household survey generates the unemployment rate from a statistically designed monthly sampling of roughly 60,000 households. Other surveys, such as the annual poverty survey, often are piggybacked on the employment questions. The survey measures the number of people who have jobs.

Payroll Survey (also **Establishment** or **Current Employment Statistics Survey**) – The payroll survey generates an estimate of the number of nonfarm jobs in the U.S. economy, based on a monthly non-random sampling of payroll tax filings of about 160,000 U.S. corporations and government agencies. The survey measures the number of jobs (some individuals hold more than one job).

The household survey is conducted during the week that includes the 12th of the month. The payroll survey is conducted as of the payroll period that includes the 12th of the month. Other than for seasonal factors, the household survey gets revised only with series or population redefinition. The payroll series is revised for two months following the initial release and then again in an annual benchmark revision.

Where the household survey includes farm workers, the self-employed and workers in private homes, the payroll survey does not. The payroll survey counts jobs, making no adjustment for multiple jobholders. Yet, adjusting for all differences, the BLS never has been able to reconcile the two series within one million jobs.

Conventional wisdom in the financial community is that the payroll survey is more accurate, given its larger sampling base. To the contrary, the household is scientifically designed, and the error can be estimated to any degree desired. The payroll data are haphazard at best, and the BLS has no idea of potential reporting error

Suggesting that the household survey is more accurate than the payroll survey, however, does not mean household survey accurately depicts unemployment. While its measures have definable statistical accuracy, the accuracy is related only to the underlying questions surveyed and to the universe of people surveyed.

The popularly followed unemployment rate was 5.5% in July 2004, seasonally adjusted. That is known as U-3, one of six unemployment rates published by the BLS. The broadest U-6 measure was 9.5%, including discouraged and marginally attached workers.

Up until the Clinton administration, a discouraged worker was one who was willing, able and ready to work but had given up looking because there were no jobs to be had. The Clinton administration dismissed to the non-reporting netherworld about five million discouraged workers who had been so categorized for more than a year. As of July 2004, the less-than-a-year discouraged workers total 504,000. Adding in the netherworld takes the unemployment rate up to about 12.5%.

The Clinton administration also reduced monthly household sampling from 60,000 to about 50,000, eliminating significant surveying in the inner cities. Despite claims of corrective statistical adjustments, reported unemployment among people of color declined sharply, and the piggybacked poverty survey showed a remarkable reversal in decades of worsening poverty trends.

Somehow, the Clinton administration successfully set into motion reestablishing the full 60,000 survey for the benefit of the current Bush administration's monthly household survey."

Source: *"GOVERNMENT ECONOMIC REPORTS: THINGS YOU'VE SUSPECTED BUT WERE AFRAID TO ASK!"* A Series Authored by Walter J. "John" Williams "Employment and Unemployment Reporting" (Part Two in a Series of Five) August 24, 2004 *http://www.shadowstats.com/article/54*

Conclusion

The foregoing information validates many people's deep scepticism regarding statistics produced by the US and other governments. The systematic fraud being perpetrated by US governments, both Democratic and Republican, in order to deceive the public about economic performance and literally rob them of billions of dollars of entitlements and pay rises is scandalous and supported by a supine media, largely owned by a handful of transnational corporations. The cynical move by the Clinton administration to remove large numbers of 'people of color' from the unemployment household survey is so typical of the amoral actions of a President who spent his Presidency having to avoid sitting down suddenly for fear of squashing the head of some Negro politician or preacher whose head was likely to be firmly lodged in his anal cavity! Whilst Bill Clinton's contemptuous attacks on Barack Obama during the 2008 battle for the Democratic nomination revealed him as the highly intelligent redneck he always was, Democratic Negroes who condemned him for attacking their new 'First Black President' were many of the same people who sat quietly by whilst their erstwhile hero oversaw the massive imprisonment of Afrikans during his two terms in office, not to mention his bombing of a baby milk factory in Sudan and attacks on Somalia. Negroes have perhaps more faith in politicians than almost any section of the US public and are happy to stand by whilst huge numbers of Afrikans and other poor people are economically raped, believing it is all in a good cause i.e. their own personal aggrandisement.

Representation without Taxation

"Only the Little People pay Taxes"
Leona Helmsley
'The Queen of Mean' who was sentenced to sixteen years imprisonment in a federal jail on tax charges. She died in 2007 leaving a $4 billion estate

A brief history of taxation

The October 2008 issue (Issue 416) of the New Internationalist magazine tells us that "The word 'tax' first appeared in the English language only in the 14th century. It derives from the Latin taxare which means 'to assess'. Before that, English used the related word 'task', derived from Old French. For a while 'task' and 'tax' were both in common use, the first requiring labour, the second money. 'Tax' then developed its meaning to imply something wearisome or challenging. So words like 'duty' were used to suggest a more appealing purpose." (New Internationalist 2008: 16) However one can go much further back into human history to find nations levying taxes. Taxes were levied in China some 3000 years ago at the birth of that nation and even further back in ancient Kemet the scribes were charged with raising funds through various forms of taxation.

Over these millennia, tax has become synonymous with economic pain on the part of the citizen or subject, however in very recent times there has been an inversion of the principle of 'progressive taxation' i.e. that the richer you are the more tax you should pay (in both absolute and relative terms); and similarly a complete flip flopping of the rallying cry for the US war of Independence against the British Crown which was 'No Taxation without Representation'. Hence the title of this chapter 'Representation without taxation', which highlights how a relatively small number of super rich individuals (and corporations) are able to exercise massive influence over the policies of governments around the world whilst paying very little in taxes.

The move to regressive tax regimes

As finance has become completely mobile with the advent of electronic banking, there has been a global race to the bottom of the taxation ladder. Countries; rich and poor, but particularly poor, have been competing to offer ever more corporation friendly tax regimes in the belief that this will attract foreign investment or retain existing large corporations that could relocate their operations elsewhere. Indeed things got so bad that in the 1990s the OECD (Organization for Economic Co-operation and Development) called for an end to the harmful competition between national tax regimes. Unfortunately, the George W Bush regime came to power and put an end to these discussions.

'Little Bush' told the US public and the world where his allegiances lay by introducing tax cutting measures in 2001 and 2003 that will "by 2012 give an average $45 a year to each of the poorest 20 per cent of Americans, and $162,000 a year to those with annual incomes of $1,million or more. In 10 years an extra $1.35 trillion would go to the American rich. " (page 6) This was all part of a pseudo-capitalistic economic policy which affirmed that the rich need tax cuts, share options and myriad financial incentives to motivate them, whilst the poor require zero hours contracts, pay cuts, longer working hours, changing shift patterns etc. to keep them motivated. I say pseudo-capitalistic because one of the hallmarks of these economic neo-cons is their belief and support for 'welfare for the rich', where government tax dollars are used to subsidise wealthy corporations and individuals. The great $12.5 trillion bailout of the banking and finance industry in the US during 2008/2009 is a classic example of this process where those who siphoned billions and perhaps trillions out of the economy are lauded in the good times and then underwritten in the bad times (which they created). Meanwhile Kwame and Ayo, along with millions of other victims of the financial crisis, who face foreclosure on their home (repossession), are left to spin on it!

One of the hallmarks of this global move towards regressive tax regimes has been the move from direct to indirect taxes. Indirect taxes are levied on things e.g. 17.5% VAT (Value Added Tax) on most consumer goods in the UK. Direct taxes are levied on people and their earnings. It is a really neat trick, if you are rich, "The poorer you are, the larger the proportion of your daily income you spend on consumption, so you pay proportionately more tax. The richer you are, the less of your wealth you pay in indirect tax – because you can never consume more than a small fraction of your income. At the very least, you probably pay no direct tax – rather than tax consultants – at all." (New Internationalist 2008: page 6)

It's a Fix

You probably have not heard of the International Accountancy Standards Board. This body is based in the City of London and is comprised of representatives of 'the Big Four' transnational accountancy firms, Deloitte Touche Tohmatsu; Pricewaterhouse Coopers; Ernst & Young and KPMG as well the Finance Directors of some of the largest corporations in the world (including Microsoft) and appointed accountancy experts. This body produces proposals on global accounting practices which are adopted as a matter of course by governments around the world. Of course the Big Four make huge profits from advising wealthy clients on how to minimise their tax liabilities and their job is made easier since they fix the rules of the game.

How the poor world is shafted

In the poor world, and Afrika in particular, much of government's income comes via the exploitation of a nation's raw materials. With the steep rise in commodity prices in recent years; one would have thought that there would have been a commensurate rise in the tax take of these poor countries. However, not so. The US and other countries of the rich world, their global financial institutions and the corporations that control international trade have a preference for direct taxes on their profits as opposed to indirect taxes on the commodities they market. You may recall that this is in complete contradiction to their view of the appropriate taxes to be levied on the individual. The reason for this volte-face? Well, it is simple really, corporations and their tax advisors are wonderfully expert at hiding profits in tax havens and using tax loopholes. One of their favourite schemes involves the mispricing of transfers between two different parts of the same corporation or between one tax haven and the next. You need to note that about "60% of world trade passes between corporate subsidiaries or havens of one sort on another....As a result, the annual revenue loss to the Majority World from transfer mispricing and tax havens now runs at an astounding $160billion a year – more than one-and-a-half times the combined development aid budgets of the rich countries in 2007....So, at the extreme, in 2006 the Democratic Republic of Congo – one of the places most richly endowed with mineral resources, most tormented by the conflicts they provoke – received a grand total of just $86,000 for mineral rights. Tanzania lost $400 million in seven years from declining royalties and taxes from mining companies." (New Internationalist 2008: 7)

Death and Taxes

This loss of taxes is not just some moot academic point. A report produced by Christian Aid entitled *Death and Taxes* indicates that at least 350,000 children under the age of five die every year as a direct result of the missing tax revenues (New Internationalist 2008 Issue 416)

Do the Maths

It is estimated that the world's super rich have stashed $11,500 billion in offshore tax havens such as Jersey, Luxembourg, Switzerland and London. This allows them to avoid paying around $250 billion each year in tax. However even this huge figure pales into relative insignificance when one considers the $1,000 to $1,600 billion per year of cross border money flows that the World Bank estimates are derived from crime, corruption and tax evasion, with half of this figure coming from the Poor World. If one weighs the foregoing numbers against the roughly $100 billion dollars that the rich countries spend on aid one can see why aid does not solve any problems, but rather just stems the blood loss a little. It is estimate that around half of the $1,000 to $1,600 billion per year of cross border money flows is due to commercial tax evasion and this is where the systematic policy of financial deregulation and weakening national tax systems is crucial. Remember the Big Four accountancy firms we spoke of earlier? Well, this is how they really earn their money, working hand in hand with their corporate clients and governments of the rich world in undermining the tax and regulatory systems around the world.

Drain the South

The flow of cash from poor to rich, South to North, Majority to Minority World is relentless. It is now also largely undocumented and untaxed. Illicit outflows, at perhaps $600 billion a year, are seven times greater than inflows of aid and double the total of foreign direct investment.

South/North financial flows[3]

Average per year 2002-06 ($ billions)

INFLOW	
Aid	84
Migrant remittances	167
Net foreign direct investment	226
New loans	380
TOTAL	**857**
OUTFLOW	
Profit remittances	130
Debt service	456
Estimated illicit flows	619
TOTAL	**1,205**
NET OUTFLOW	**348**

www.newint.org

Source: *New Internationalist* October 2008 page 13

Derivatives – The $1,000,000,000,000,000 Elephant in the Room

As I was in the process of writing this chapter, in early October 2008, the various branches of the US government were putting the final touches to their Wall Street 'bailout' plan. After being initially rejected by the House of Representatives; the $700 billion of taxpayers' money was boosted to $850 billion with $150 billion of sweeteners added that would assist the legislators' favourite industrial sectors. When the deal was done the elected officials gathered on Capitol Hill to verbally slap each other on the back and praise the 'bipartisan' effort that had brought this 'historic' deal to a successful conclusion.

Now, given the nearly infantile level of information communicated to the general public by the corporate owned media, one could have been forgiven for thinking that this nationalisation of private, corporate debt would have some fundamental impact upon the level of 'toxic debt' circulating in the US financial markets. If only that were true, however it is far from the case. In order that you, the reader, has a better insight into the incredible, unserviceable level of indebtedness that is an integral part of the current US dominated global economic system, I need to deal with the subject of derivatives, because when you understand what derivatives are and how they work you will see that the $850 billion bailout is just a drop in the ocean of global financial debt and is like throwing bad money after bad.

What are Derivatives?

Ellen Brown in her article *It's The Derivatives, Stupid! Why Fannie, Freddie, AIG Had To Be Bailed Out* (20 September, 2008 *webofdebt.com*), tells us that,

"Derivatives are financial instruments that have no intrinsic value but derive their value from something else. Basically, they are just bets. You can "hedge your bet" that something you own will go up by placing a side bet that it will go down. "Hedge funds" hedge bets in the derivatives market. Bets can be placed on anything, from the price of tea in China to the movements of specific markets.

"The point everyone misses," wrote economist Robert Chapman a decade ago, "is that buying derivatives is not investing. It is gambling, insurance and high stakes bookmaking. Derivatives create nothing."[1] They not only create nothing, but they serve to enrich non-producers at the expense of the people who do create real goods and services. In congressional hearings in the early 1990s, derivatives trading was challenged as being an illegal form of gambling. But the practice was legitimized by Fed Chairman Alan Greenspan, who not only lent legal and regulatory support to the trade but actively promoted derivatives as a way to improve "risk management". Partly, this was to boost the flagging profits of the banks; and at the larger banks and dealers, it worked. But the cost was an increase in risk to the financial system as a whole." (Brown 2008)

How much is gambled on derivatives?

Brown goes on to tell us that "derivative trades have grown exponentially, until now they are larger than the entire global economy. The Bank for International Settlements recently reported that total derivatives trades exceeded one quadrillion dollars – that's 1,000 trillion dollars. How is that figure even possible? The gross domestic product of all the countries in the world is only about 60 trillion dollars. The answer is that gamblers can bet as much as they want. They can bet money they don't have, and that is where the huge increase in risk comes in." (Brown 2008)

A ticking time bomb

Now everything is fine until the house of cards begins to collapse. Credit Default Swaps (CDS), the most widely traded form of credit derivatives are like insurance policies in many ways, in which one party buys protection against a company defaulting on its bonds from another company. However the company buying protection does not actually have to – and most often does not – actually hold any asset or suffer any loss if the company defaults. It's just a high stakes gamble.

However things can get tricky if the company that is gambled on does default. This can leave the 'protection seller' with a liability of let's say $100 million in claims. Now the hedge fund may simply put the corporate shell or limited partnership used to conduct the transaction into bankruptcy, however they set off a chain reaction as they have to write off the derivatives which were listed as assets on their accounts and those gamblers who cannot collect on their winning bets because of the default, now default on their losing bets, which causes other gamblers to default, and so on.

Brown notes that "The potential for this sort of nuclear reaction was what prompted billionaire investor Warren Buffett to call derivatives 'weapons of financial mass destruction'. It is also why the banking system cannot let a major derivatives player go down, and it is the banking system that calls the shots. The Federal Reserve is literally owned by a conglomerate of banks; and Hank Paulson, who heads the U.S. Treasury, entered that position through the revolving door of investment bank Goldman Sachs, where he was formerly CEO." (Brown 2008)

When the smelly stuff hits the fan

Many readers will remember the quasi nationalisation of those oddly named financial institutions, Fannie Mae and Freddie Mac. Now, the public was led to believe that the motivation was simply to save those huge mortgage companies, however in fact the mortgage liabilities of these companies were not the real reason. This rescue was put together to prevent a $1.4 trillion "event of default" which would have hit the derivatives industry in the event of the two mortgage giants collapsing. In this scenario the value of the endangered bonds drops by 70% causing $1 trillion (70% of $1.4 trillion) to be due to the "protection buyers". This is more money than the "protection sellers" can afford. This leads to a sudden loss of confidence of their creditors who withdraw lines of credit leading to a cascade of cross-defaults "until nearly every major investment bank and commercial bank is unable to meet its obligations. This triggers another massive round of CDS events, going to $10 trillion, then $20 trillion. The financial centers become insolvent, the markets have to be shut down, and when they open months later, the stock market has been crushed.

The federal government and the financiers pulling its strings naturally feel compelled to step in to prevent such a disaster, even though this rewards the profligate speculators at the expense of the Fannie/Freddie shareholders who will get wiped out." (Brown 2008)

It is because this whole system is built on sand that these super rich corporate gamblers operate in a heads I win tails the taxpayer loses world. The government simply cannot afford not to bail them out at the expense of 99.9% of the population. So be assured, whether it is in another ten years, fifteen years or twenty years we will see another similar crisis and whilst the details may be different, the fundamentals of an economy built upon unserviceable debt and wild speculation will be the same.

SECTION II

The role of Culture & Psychology in Wealth Creation

There is a hole in our bucket – The Local Multiplier effect

In attempting to maximise economic resources the ability to keep money circulating in the community is of vital importance. The more times money goes around, the wealthier your community will be. However, it is not just where you spend your money that counts, but also where the people you give it to spend it... and so on. This is the *'local multiplier effect'* the net effect of spending patterns. In this chapter we are going to look at money flows which are affected by not only a local community's – be it a geographic or ethnic community – income level, but perhaps more importantly their culture and group psychology and degree of cohesiveness. The tighter knit and stronger their bonds of loyalty and kinship the more they will restrict their spending to within their group and vice versa. Of course in order to be able to spend within your own community your community needs to be able to produce relevant goods and services and of course this is also linked to group culture, values, customs and attitudes.

The New Economics Foundation (NEF) in the UK has done some excellent work around explaining how local economies work and creating tools to assist local people to take greater control over their economic lives. In their highly informative and practical publication; *'Plugging the Leaks – Making the most of every pound that enters your local economy'* (Ward & Lewis 2002), they provide two clear examples of the local multiplier effect in action.

The first relates to a study of Tayside in the UK which showed that tourists who stayed in Bed & Breakfast accommodation brought greater local economic benefits than those who stayed in hotels even though the latter group spent on average 70% more than people staying in B & Bs. The reason for this was because most of the money spent in hotels immediately leaked out of the local economy in the shape of non-local staff and owners, services provided by non-local firms and so on.

The second and even starker example relates to a small, predominately Afrikan, district of Baltimore, USA. This community is characterised by extremely high levels of unemployment after the closure of traditional heavy industries. Virtually all the money that comes into the community, predominantly in the shape of welfare payments (social security), is immediately spent outside the community at discount food stores. There is no recycling or re-circulation of money and locals estimate that the 'local multiplier effect' is exactly 1.0. The NEF publication compares this multiplier score with the community development corporation target circulation of 8, which they reckon is the average for a predominantly white, predominantly employed suburb in the USA.

The following example taken from the same NEF publication shows you how to calculate the 'local multiplier effect'.

Let us look at transactions in two given communities. In community A 80% of money is retained on average, whereas in community B only 20% of money is retained per transaction. Some of the calculations have been rounded up to the nearest whole figure.

Community A (£) 80%		Community B (£) 20%	
Enters	Remains	Enters	Remains
100	80	100	20
80	64	20	4
64	51	4	1
51	41	1	
41	33		
33			
Total = **500**		Total = **125**	
Multiplier = 500/100 = **5**		Multiplier = 125/100 = **1.25**	

After just three transactions Community A ends up with approximately 51 times more money left to continue circulating in the community than community B. See it deh!

Community activists need to understand this principle, teach it to others, and then; and most importantly, work with the community to plug the leaks in the local economic bucket. Afrikans in the United States have an estimated total annual spending power of $760billion (Target Marketing 2006), however the vast majority of this is frittered away and handed on a golden platter to competitor ethnic groups. Similarly, in the UK the annual spend of Afrikans runs into the billions of pounds and likewise this money is poured into an economic bucket with more holes than bucket. This was why the

ABDF (see later in this book) was set up and this is an absolute essential priority to be tackled if Afrikans are to get off our collective economic arses. Scene!

Economic Irrigation

If we conceive of our local community as farmland suffering from a moderate shortage of rain we need to think of how we can bring in additional water to increase the productivity of the land. We can do this by constructing an irrigation channel, however this will only increase the fertility of the land on the banks of the channel as can be seen by looking at the land on the left hand side of the diagram. However if we create additional channels running off the main channel we can dramatically increase the area of fertile irrigated land.

The foregoing analogy gives us a way of thinking of inward investment into an economically deprived area. This investment could come from a private corporation or more likely government regeneration money. The immediate direct impact of this inward investment will be felt by the local people employed as a result of this investment and their families. However if we really want to spread the benefits we need to encourage those people newly employed to spend their money with local businesses, encourage local businesses and public bodies to employ local people and source their supplies locally as well as encouraging local people to save money through activities such as energy conservation schemes, food co-ops, LETS (Local Economic Trading Systems) etc.

Our Holey Bucket

So once we have established a steady flow of money into our community we have the difficult task of ensuring that the money is recycled as much as possible before it leaks out. The New Economics Foundation uses the analogy of a leaky bucket to highlight the type of rapid leaking of money experienced by poor communities as exemplified by the Local Multiplier Effect.

The African-Caribbean community in the UK and the African-American community are two examples of Afrikan communities that are almost obsessively concerned with money inflows (earnings/regeneration money) and which pay precious little attention to money outflows e.g. with whom they spend their money, who the recipients of their money employ, co-operative activity to reduce food, energy and other costs etc.

The diagrams below exemplify this problem.

In some of our communities we don't even have the luxury of worrying about leaks since the money almost seems to hit the community and bounce away without anyone being able to get hold of it. NEF highlight the example of contracts awarded to improve housing. As they note:

"The contracts almost always go to external contractors, because they have the experience of delivering to high standards, tight timescales and so on.

The leaky bucket

'There are so many holes in our local economy you could even say we didn't have a bucket at all!'

Bob from NEF's Boncath workshop

Imagine your economy as a bucket. The money that comes into your area will flow straight out again if there are many holes in the bucket. A full bucket means that local people have enough money to be able to buy what they need for a good quality of life. But if your bucket is leaky then to fill the bucket you will need to pour the money in at a faster rate than it is pouring out. So there are two strategies to fill a bucket – you can pour in the money faster, or you can slow down its leakage by plugging some of the leaks.

In economic terms that means you both focus on attracting more money into your area – inward investment, grants, welfare benefits, export sales and so on. And you slow down the rate of leakage through local sourcing, adding value locally, using local resources. We've become so obsessed with bringing in new money that this second strategy for economic development has recently been neglected. That's why it forms the focus of this handbook.

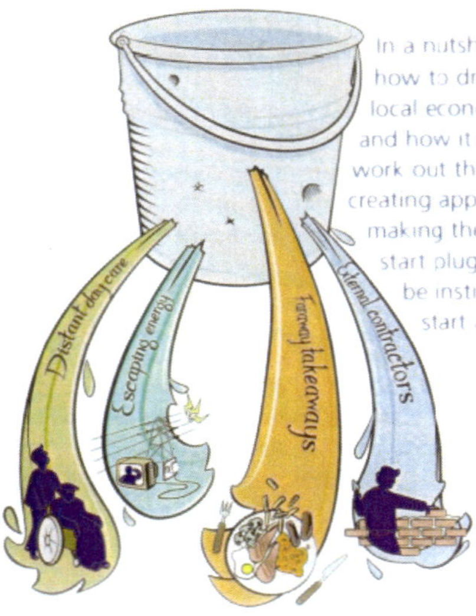

In a nutshell, the Plugging the Leaks workshop explains how to draw a picture of the leaky bucket for your own local economy – showing how money currently pours in and how it currently leaks out. The next step is to roughly work out the scale of the different leaks, the ease of creating appropriate plugs and how interested people are in making the plug. It is then relatively straightforward to start plugging some leaks. It is also an approach that can be instinctively understood by people so that they can start applying the logic to all aspects of their lives.

Source: *Plugging the Leaks* (Ward & Lewis 2002: 17)

... a better approach for the local economy would be to create a funnel for the funding so that more of it could stay in the community. In practical terms this would mean undertaking the work more slowly, gradually supporting the strengthening of capacity inside the community so that they are able to undertake their own development. For example, a scheme could be created to strengthen relevant building skills in the first couple of years of a regeneration programme. Then those trainees could form the basis for local tenders for contracts in subsequent years - though clearly they will need to win such contracts on the basis of open competition." (Ward & Lewis 2002: 21-22)

The foregoing discussion can be broadened to consideration of inward investment into Afrikan countries by foreign nation states or corporations. Once again we see the failure to develop local capacity as with much of the current wave of Chinese investment into Afrika which normally involves large scale infrastructure projects delivered by Chinese companies using Chinese labour. The Afrikan countries get roads, railways, electrification, power plants etc. And the Chinese get the energy supplies and raw materials such as copper, coltan, uranium, zinc, gold, etc. which are needed to fuel their rapidly expanding economy.

Whilst these construction projects definitely bring short and medium term benefits, how will these countries be able to maintain this infrastructure without the creation of local capacity? Or will they end up like the numerous grand houses of the colonial period that can be found in so many Afrikan cities and that have fallen into disrepair with insufficient resources and skilled personnel available for their upkeep?

Spending Circles

If we imagine our local Afrikan community as at the centre of circles where the outside circle represents non-Afrikan communities, the second circle representing non-local Afrikan communities either in the UK or abroad and the inner circle your local Afrikan community in the town or city you live, then we want to move from the situation on the left where we spend the majority of our money with non-Afrikans to the situation on the right where we spend as much possible with our own people who are most likely to reinvest in our community.

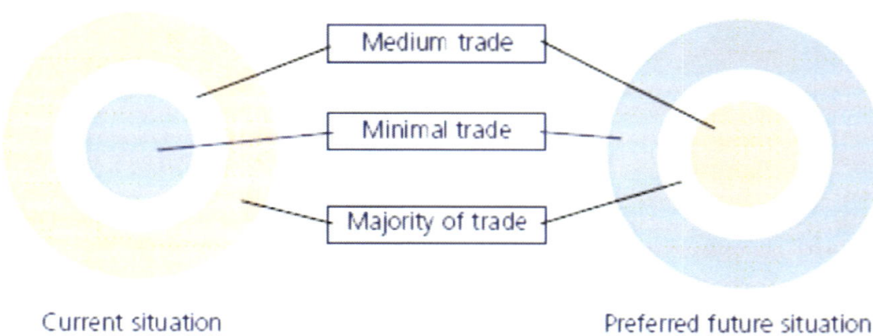

Sources of Income

The diagram below highlights that Black people in the UK "are the most dependent of all communities on wages and salaries for their income (i.e. White 65%, Indian 70%, Pakistani/Bangladeshi 35%, Black 74%)." (Kwaw, Page 10, The Whirlwind, Issue 3, 2006)

What is perhaps even more instructive is to look at the relative amounts of household income derived from Self-employment income. Here we see that the percentage for Afrikans is this time the lowest and by a significant amount, coming in at less than 10% as compared to Whites where well over 20% of income is derived from self-employment and Pakistanis/Bangladeshis where the figure is virtually 40%.

Indians come in at just under 20%, however they have a far greater proportion of people employed in professional/managerial positions, earning higher level incomes and therefore experiencing greater job and financial security. This can be contrasted with the position of Black people in the UK where over 40% of our work force are on low incomes (Kwaw, Page 10, The Whirlwind, Issue 3, 2006).

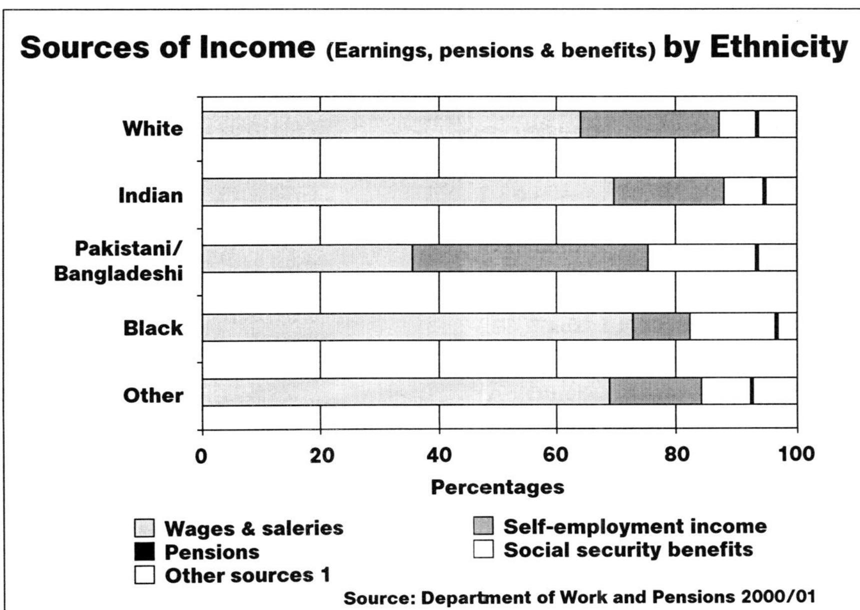

The old adage of *'get an education and get a good job'* handed down to us through the generations has to be quietly and unceremoniously buried and replaced with something along the lines of *'develop the skills and knowledge that will enable you to always be in a position to take care of yourself, your family and your community'*.

I gave up working for other people on 1st February 2006 and Creator willing I will never go back to employment again.

PERSONAL ATTITUDES AND GROUP PSYCHOLOGY

It is widely recognised by Afrikans across a wide range of ideological positions that we need to increase the number and range of Afrikan owned businesses and to increase the size of existing Afrikan owned businesses. This is necessary for a number of reasons including:

- To create wealth that can be retained and redistributed within the Afrikan domestic economy and not repatriated to foreign countries or foreign groups. This wealth can be used to provide clean water, primary health care, adequate food supplies and build infrastructure.
- To create jobs. It has been suggested that each year the Afrikan continent needs to create at least 10 million jobs just to stand still employment wise i.e. to absorb the net new entrants to the labour market.
- To heal the psychological scars of conquest, enslavement and colonisation. A people locked into beggardom can never be free.

Whilst there are many structural barriers that help to keep Afrikan people impoverished – which we shall touch on later – There are also psychological and cultural barriers to business development and wealth creation which have to be addressed.

George Subira in his often overlooked book 'Black Folks guide to Business Success' identifies 11 'Black attitudes' to wealth creation that he feels impedes business success. Whilst he does not suggest that these attitudes are exclusive to Afrikan people in the US, he does suggest that they are disproportionately common amongst Afrikans. I would suggest that some of these same attitudes are common amongst Afrikans in Canada, the Caribbean and UK and also in Afrika. These attitudes are:

1. **Black People are a Poor People.** Subira suggests that tied up in this belief is the fact that Black people are generally very poor money managers whilst being very 'brand

conscious' and spending disproportionately on conspicuous consumer items. This contributes to our 'poverty cycle'. He also suggests that many Black leaders have seen it in their interest to push this poverty angle in order to squeeze more jobs and concessions from their White masters. If this attitude was successfully addressed he suggests we would be more creative in coming up with solutions to our problems and more of us would go into business when we realise that our community is not poor. Obviously there are real issues of extreme and widespread income poverty for our people in Afrika and other parts of the poor world.

2. **Money Is the Root of All Evil, or The Love of Money is the Root of All Evil.** At the time of writing his book (1986) Subira suggested that the biggest institution in the Afrikan community in the US, the Church, was "the most powerful force which programs us against money..." (Subira 1986: 53) Since that time we have seen the rise of prosperity ministries, which have crossed over from the Caucasian community to the Afrikan community, most notably led by ministers such as Kreflo Dollar who certainly seems to live up to his name, collecting over $60 million in donations in one year. Some of these prosperity churches have installed the technology to accept credit and debit cards during services! Notwithstanding this new volte-face by elements of the Black church there still remains a strong element which promotes the idea that to be poor is to be pure.

3. **Money is Only Possible Through the Exploitation of Other People.** I don't often quote Jesse Jackson, however I believe it was him who said "Just because you have been victimised it does not mean that you have to act like a victim." Because of our more recent history of holding the blade whilst others hold the handle, as a people we are very rightly sensitive to the idea of exploitation, and it seems particularly sensitive to being exploited by other

Afrikans. However as Subira points out "Black victims of America have to escape the victim's point of view if they are to be economically and spiritually free. .."(Subira 1986: 55)

4. **You have Got to Have Money to Make Money.** Subira suggests that this is a half truth i.e. that it is "true no more than half the time. It only takes two things to make money in America: having the ability to sell and having something to sell." (Subira 1986: 55) Linked to this latter idea he suggests that the negative attitude of Black people in America to selling has severely impaired their ability to make money and create wealth.
5. **White Folks are Not going to Let Black People Make Any Real Money.** Subira suggests that the psychology underpinning this attitude is rooted in: the idea that Whites will always have dominative power over Blacks, an ignorance of the present US reality that many Black millionaires are paid directly by Whites (often in the field of entertainment where Whites are the billionaires!) and ignorance as to how big money is made. As Subira says "We will get what we want when we decide we want it not when somebody decides to give it to us." (Subira 1986: 59)
6. **I Don't Need Money to Enjoy Life (Money is Only For Material Things).** This idea Subira suggests is linked to the limited perception that money should be used for personal consumption. However a wider view would recognise that money can not only be used to satisfy ones material needs and wants but also for other uses such as to invest in the business ideas of other Afrikan entrepreneurs, to support good causes such as education healthcare, the arts etc. It takes money to develop new goods and services and Afrikans need to become producers.
7. **Money Weakens Your Character, Makes You Soft and Spoils an Otherwise Good Human Being.** This attitude is

similar to number 6 in that it is linked to the idea that money is only for, or mainly for consumption, whereas money can also be the means to bring your ideas to fruition and to improve the world. If we apply the 'law of flip' (Grant 2005) then as Subira notes "The idea of money weakening one's character or making one soft or spoiled suggests that poverty would do the opposite. Does poverty strengthen one's Character?" (Subira 1986: 61)

8. **Religious and Political Fatalism.** Religious fatalists are obsessed with 'the end is nigh' and life after death, hence see very little need to address the fundamental inequities of society but rather to focus on individual piety so as to be assured of their place in heaven. The other fatalists are those who predict the imminent fall of the 'Western' economies; hence since these economies are about to fall there is no point in trying to build up businesses, assets and wealth. The irony is that most of these people work for government (local or central) or the voluntary sector (funded by government or grants from charitable trusts endowed by large corporations). If you offer most of these people a practical opportunity to engage in collective economics they will raise some objection, if you ask them what co-operative economic entity they have created they normally have little but theory to offer.

9. **You Just End Up Paying More In Taxes.** This attitude is partly rooted in a mindset I call *'learned helplessness'* in which the 'victim' is unable to believe in their own capacity to effect significant change in their life and when presented with viable solutions to real problems manage to convince themself that the solution will only lead to a problem of similar magnitude to that of the original problem. As Subira puts it "Making money does not mean much to them because they believe there is no way that they could hold onto it even if they made it." (Subira 1986: 64)

10. **I'm Too Old Now to Make Any Money.** As George Subira points out sometimes we are not ready, either for psychological, experiential or financial reasons to start a business until we are more mature (perhaps when children are grown up) and it would be a shame for restrictive belief systems to stop us from seizing these business opportunities with both hands just because we don't conform to the age profile of the 'typical' new business owner.
11. **The Super Star Syndrome.** This attitude highlights the hypocrisy and double standards of much of the Afrikan community. Subira points out how whilst superstar athletes and entertainers are allowed to get away with the most irresponsible and degenerate behaviour and experience little negative reaction from the Afrikan community, those Afrikan businesspeople who actually work in and serve their people are the subject of constant scrutiny and criticism for relatively minor misdemeanours and are expected to 'give back' to their people to a much greater extent than the generally much richer Negro entertainers. No 'ordinary' Afrikan paedophile/sexual predator could have behaved as Michael Jackson and R Kelly have done and received so much support from Afrikan people. If I professed to habitually sleeping with little boys I don't think Afrikan people would have extended me the same level of understanding or made up the same ridiculous excuses to explain my behaviour as in the case of Jacko. Neither would they be offering to send their children to stay at my house as some Negroes did with Jackson. If we poured half the opprobrium onto wayward superstars that we pour on to 'ordinary' people who achieve business success and extended half the understanding to ordinary people that we extend to superstars it might pay us better.

CORRUPTION – The Great Unmentionable

The issue of corruption falls partially under the heading of institutional causes of impoverishment, however I think fundamentally it best fits under the cultural heading with recognition being given to the importance of how poverty increases the likelihood of corruption.

It appears to me that corruption in Afrika is another one of those Pan-Afrikanist holy cows, like the Continentalist version of Pan-Afrikanism or the belief that reparations is going to solve our economic problems. If one raises the issue of corruption the immediate response is to highlight corruption in 'the West', as if two wrongs make a right and yet anyone who moves beyond this reflexive; defensive position knows that there is a serious problem with corruption in many Afrikan countries.

Some of this defensiveness and hostility towards anyone who raises the issue of corruption in Afrika is I believe connected to these people being stuck in what Oba T'Shaka refers to in his book 'The Integration Trap: The Generation Gap' (2005) as the 'Romantic Stage' of Afrikan identity. In this work he describes the following stages of identity formation for Afrikans:

- The Stage of Negro Identity
- The Stage of Pre-Disturbance
- The Stage of Disturbance
- The Stage of African Identity
- The Withdrawal Stage
- The Romantic Stage
- Balanced Self-Appraisal
- The Self Inventory Stage
- The Life, Death Rebirth Stage
- The Revolutionary African Identity Stage

T'Shaka suggests that *"the romantic phase is the time where you see only good in your African ...past and only bad in European history and culture. While the Negro believed that white was good, the awakened African during the romantic phase too often thinks that whites are all bad, and Blacks are all good. Although this appraisal is unbalanced it is absolutely necessary to correct the previous negative self-concept... Romantic love does not last forever. Eventually, you come to realize that the object of your affections has both positive and negative qualities. In the same way, the romantic phase of historical and cultural immersion ends when the awakened person realizes that African civilisations and African culture had both positive and negative qualities... When we reach the stage in studying our history where we see the positives and negatives in our past, it is absolutely essential that we distinguish one aspect from the other. We have to do this so that we can internalize those positive values that still have relevance to us and that we need for own growth and development. We must face the negatives in our historical past and work to discard them, so that we do not end up being them."* (T'Shaka 2005: 49-51)

Those of us based in 'the West' will have to discard our rose tinted glasses if are to avoid severe disappointment and if we are to fulfil our potential and make a serious and vital contribution to an economic renaissance in Afrika.

As I have mentioned in previous books I conceived of the Afrikan Business Development Fund (ABDF) in 1996 and co-founded it later that year. The ABDF Ltd has started investing in Ghana – which is not one of the most corrupt countries in Afrika – and our Manager in Ghana, who has been visiting and investing there since 1999 and who is now permanently based there; has told us clearly of his and others experience of doing business there. Apart from the inevitable cultural differences, he is quite unequivocal that Ghana is a *'grease palm'* country. This does not mean that everyone is corrupt, it does however mean that fairly straightforward administrative tasks undertaken by government agencies and civil servants which could be completed in a few weeks, not only take much longer, but also often require the greasing of palms to expedite the process from interminable to very slow.

This kind of entrenched corruption acts as a barrier and disincentive to investment. In his book 'The Undercover Economist'

Tim Harford reflects on the mountain of bureaucratic red tape that is stymieing the development of the Cameroonian economy. "...but there are metaphorical roadblocks throughout the Cameroonian economy. The World Bank threw light on them when it recently started collecting data about simple business regulations. The Bank discovered that in order to set up a small business, an entrepreneur in Cameroon must spend on official fees nearly as much as the average Cameroonian makes in two years....To buy and sell property costs nearly a fifth of the property's value. To get the courts to enforce an unpaid invoice takes nearly two years, costs over a third of the invoice's value and requires fifty eight separate procedures. These ridiculous procedures are good news for the bureaucrats who enforce them. Every procedure is an opportunity to extract a bribe. The slower the standard processes, the greater is the temptation to pay 'speed money'." (Harford 2007: 190)

"In a similar vein he notes that "after the World Bank advertised the fact that entrepreneurs in Ethiopia couldn't legally start a business without paying four years salary to publish an official notice in government newspapers, the Ethiopian government relented and decided to scrap the regulation. New business registrations jumped by almost 50 per cent immediately." (Harford 2007: 191)

It should be noted that Tim Harford is a neo-liberal economist and of course the World Bank is no friend of Afrika. However from the World Bank's perspective some lies are worth telling and some are not. The type of issues raised by the World Bank and cited by Tim Harford, in terms of business regulation, are easily refuted by Governments and hence the World Bank is less likely to lie about them.

I need to make it clear that I am not underestimating the widespread nature of corruption in the Caucasian world. I have seen it at first hand in the UK, in a political, financial and moral sense. The following items highlight corruption in the Caucasian world.

I was watching a programme, Working Lunch, on the BBC on 28 April 2008 and the presenter was interviewing Nigel Farrage, the leader of, UKIP (UK Independence Party) a small political party which wants the UK to leave the European Union (EU). Mr Farrage highlighted the long running scandal surrounding the expenses claimed by Members of the European Parliament (MEP). After many years of widespread and widely suspected fraud, the EU finally conducted an investigation into these expenses. This was only the beginning of the saga as there was then a protracted battle as the MEPs fought to keep the findings of the investigation secret, reminiscent of the 2009 scandal over the expenses of UK Members of Parliament.

The following article by David Charter from the Times Newspaper online on 21 February 2008 gives you a flavour of the scandal.

MEPs 'expenses abuse' hushed up by Brussels

"A secret internal inquiry by the European Parliament has found widespread abuse of expenses by MEPs employing fictitious staff or unqualified family members, it was revealed last night.

Europe's anti-fraud watchdog has launched an investigation after learning about the audit which was kept under wraps by the parliament and only shown to MEPs on request at a secret location — and even then they were not allowed to make notes, only read the damning report.

The explosive inquiry centres on misuse of the annual parliamentary assistants allowance of £130,000 available to all 785 MEPs to pay staff — a total of more than £100 million.

It found malpractice by many MEPs in a random sample that showed some of them claimed the cash for fictitious staff or unqualified family members in an echo of the Tory MP who lost the Conservative whip last month for employing his undergraduate son.

The EU's independent investigation team was called in by Chris Davies, the Liberal Democrat MEP, who said: "This report is dynamite — and makes the Derek Conway affair at Westminster look like small-change." Mr Davies is one of a group of MEPs on the European Parliament's Budget Control Committee who were allowed to look at the report this week. Committee members were also supposed to sign a confidentiality agreement.

But Mr Davies did not, and last night he revealed that the auditors' catalogue of alleged abuses of payments for MEPs' office staff for the audited period between late 2004 and early 2006. "When I looked at this report my first reaction was to laugh at the outrageous extent of the abuses" said Mr Davies.

"Then that feeling turned to anger and the realisation that the police or the anti-fraud people should be looking at this." Mr Davies said that many MEPs seem to be involved in malpractice, with large sums of money impossible to account for, according to the audit report. But the document names no names and leaves major questions over how MEP staff allowances have been used.

Most MEPs use an established payment system, which involves appointing a "service provider" — a professional accountancy firm or other professional book-keeper — to handle all cash destined for parliamentary staff.

According to Mr Davies this system is revealed as giving MEPs plenty of freedom to conceal the true extent of payment and recipients.

Mr Davies said that the report reveals that, in some cases, the "service providers" are fictitious. In other cases MEPs employ no official staff, and sometimes social security payments required under Belgian law are not paid. In one case staff working for one MEP received a Christmas bonus 19 times of monthly salary.

The report is due to be discussed by the European Parliament's Budget Control Committee on Tuesday: "Maybe when some MEPs are exposed for defrauding Parliament and are sent to prison a more acceptable approach will be adopted," Mr Davies said.

So there it is, corruption at the heart of the EU and as was noted in the above article there was a similar scandal brewing in the British Parliament concerning Members of Parliament (MPs) employing their relatives using their expenses. In some cases these family members are carrying out legitimate work on behalf of the MP, whilst in other cases it is just a scam to siphon taxpayer money into the family coffers. Of course since this article was written the UK Parliamentary expenses scandal has blown wide open.

In my book *'Blue Skies for Afrikans'* (2005) I highlighted Jeffrey St Clair's book *'Grand Theft Pentagon'* which reveals how huge government contracts to rebuild/restore Iraqi infrastructure, destroyed by the US invasion were being carved up in smoke filled rooms and divvied up between huge US corporations, often without any competitive tendering process, in what they call 'no bid contracts'. In Blue Skies for Afrikans I detailed how US corporation, Kellog Brown & Root (KBR) – a subsidiary of the giant Haliburton corporation, of which US Vice President Dick Cheney was formerly Vice-President of the Board – was given a $7billion contract as part of the Restore Iraqi Oil (RIO) programme without having to face any competition from other companies qualified to deliver the work. When this piece of malfeasance was investigated by Bunnatine 'Bunny' Greenhouse, a high ranking civilian in the Army Corps of Engineers, she was subject to trumped up disciplinary investigations and eventual demotion after an unblemished employment record with the Corps of over 20 years.

I think one of the major issues in relation to issues of corruption and bureaucracy in Afrika and 'the West' relates to at what level it occurs and how it occurs. What I mean by this can be related to the example of setting up a business cited earlier. In Cameroon, as we have seen, there is a huge financial disadvantage to setting up an official business and hence many entrepreneurs don't bother and hence don't pay taxes, reducing government receipts and their ability to invest in health, education etc. When I set up a limited company in the UK in 2006, I employed an accountant, paid them about £400 and they carried out all of the administration and form filling, save me signing a few forms and returning them back to them. In a few weeks I received my certificate from Companies House as proof of the successful formation of my company. It never crossed my mind that I would have to pay 'speed money', remortgage my house to be able to afford it or wait for several months for the process to be completed.

The administration of these types of routine tasks such as business formation, passport applications etc. is generally much quicker, straightforward and cheaper (in relative terms) in richer countries than in poor ones such as Cameroon. Part of the problem is that civil servants in countries such as Cameroon are extremely poorly paid whereas in the UK by comparison they are relatively well paid. This poverty will lead to corruption in an environment where there is widespread political corruption from the top downwards such as in Cameroon.

This type of routine corruption is not only bad for business it is bad for the functioning of almost every type of activity. It disincentivises educational achievement since jobs are given out based on nepotism and leads to a vicious cycle of ever more entrenched corruption. In 'the West' corruption is actually more widespread the higher one goes up the socio-economic ladder. It is on a huge level, however, and this is important, it does not regularly impede the conduct of routine government administration, rather it is more about insider trading, jobs for the boys, lobbying and political funding in return for favourable legislation and generally welfare for the rich and corporations.

This widespread corruption and inordinate bureaucracy in many Afrikan countries is a significant barrier to investment by Afrikans in the Diaspora who, hearing horror stories from Afrikans who have tried to buy land or build houses, feel trepidation at the prospect of investing, let alone repatriation. Part of this fear is due to negative stereotypes, part is due to a lack of reliable contacts on the ground and part is due to the issues of corruption I have raised in this chapter.

We cannot keep on burying our heads in the sand and pretend that corruption is not a real issue that must be tackled head on in Afrika. In China in 2007 several senior government officials were executed for their part in a scheme to manufacture and sell fake pharmaceuticals. When was the last we heard of senior officials in an

Afrikan government facing such serious consequences for corruption? If you don't tackle corruption at the top it is almost impossible to make any headway lower down the 'food chain', particularly where poverty is widespread. When I was in Gambia in 2007, we were travelling in a jeep and were stopped by the police. The pretext was that the jeep was overloaded; however the real motivation was not to issue a ticket, but rather to extort a bribe from the brothers who were taking us on our excursion. Bribes are like unregulated, unpredictable taxes and create barriers to social, economic, political and spiritual development.

Whilst there is much emphasis placed upon the role of the corrupted in Afrika and other parts of the world there is much less discussion of the role of the corruptors i.e. the transnational corporations who view corruption as a routine part of business practice.

In identifying the increasing drive for overseas profits by US multinationals James Petras notes:

"The principal new targets of MNCs, banks, pension funds and institutional investors are the 'BRIC' countries – Brazil, Russia, India and China.....What is striking about the 'BRIC' countries and their growing attraction for US and EU MNCs is their extremely poor rating with regard to corruption. There is a strong correlation between the 'attractiveness' of the 'BRIC' countries and the ease of doing business and having access to highly lucrative economic enterprises and sectors once the political leaders have been paid off." (Petras 2007 54-55)

Petras goes on to highlight how corruption is widely accepted as an everyday part of business practice by the leaders of these corporations.

"According to a six-country survey of 350 corporations published by the law firm, Control Risks and Simmons and Simmons, "a third of international companies think they failed to win new business over the past year because of bribery by their competitors". Moreover most MNCs and banks engage in corrupt practices through intermediaries. If we include direct and indirect forms of corporate corruption then it turns out that in some countries 9 out of 10 corporations engage in corruption. According to the survey, "about three quarters of the companies, including 94 per cent in Germany and 90 per cent in Britain think businesses from their countries use agents to circumvent anti-corruption laws"." (Petras 2007: 56)

Therefore we can see that corruption is not a one way street as often portrayed, with high principled executives of transnational corporations being 'forced' to pay bribes by corrupt leaders. It is a mutually reinforcing and beneficial relationship, with the only losers being the literally billions of people in the poor(er) countries targeted for exploitation.

We will now turn to look at internal systemic corruption within the United States. Stephen Lendman in an article entitled 'Barack Obama: Crime Boss' on the Countercurrents.org website tells us that:

"Economics Professor William Black is a former senior bank regulator and Savings and Loan prosecutor, currently teaching economics and law at the University of Missouri. In an April 13 Barrons interview, he referred to "failed bankers (advising) failed regulators on how to deal with failed assets" they all had a hand in creating and proliferating.

He called the scale of financial fraud "immense", and said "Unless the current administration changes course pretty drastically, the scandal will destroy Barack Obama's presidency," besides what it's doing to the country, global economies, and many millions of people here and abroad.

He scathed Summers and Geithner, both "important architects of (today's) problems," and the latter as a failed and dishonest regulator, yet "numbering himself among those who convey tough medicine when he's really pandering to the interests of a select group of banks." No need to mention which ones.

The law mandates corrective action, the kind FDR took in the 1930s. He, Bernanke and Summers flout the law, "in naked violation, in order to pursue the kind of favoritism that the law was designed to prevent." They've turned taxpayers into "suckers" who'll pay dearly for decades, maybe generations.

His refusal to put insolvent banks into receivership, resorting to deceptive language like "legacy assets", and pursuing the worst of Chicago School economics "is positively Orwellian....If cheaters prosper, (they'll) dominate. It's like Gresham's law: Bad money drives out the good. Well, bad behavior" does the same thing "without good enforcement."........

With most, perhaps all, the big banks insolvent (a polite term for bankrupt), what's going on is "a multi-trillion dollar cover-up by publicly traded (enterprises), which amounts to felony securities fraud on a massive scale.".......

What's needed is a 1930s-style Pecora investigation to get to the bottom of their fraud, deceit, and cover-up, along with government complicity to hide it. .....

Black cited billions to AIG as the single worst abuse so far - to bail out their counterparties like Switzerland's UBS at the same time we were prosecuting it for tax fraud. As bad was following Goldman Sachs' advice to direct a $13 billion counterparty windfall to itself.

The whole process reeks of corruption. It must be stopped, and a new direction instituted under a reformist economic team - one that will admit the nature and depth of the problem, cut the tie to Wall Street, and take corrective action the law mandates. That's "precisely what isn't happening." (Lendman 19 April 2009)

In this chapter we have looked at corruption amongst Afrikan governments, corruption within the European Union and amongst the Members of the European Parliament and corruption in the US government in relation to its relationships with Wall Street financial institutions. In all cases this corruption, be it petty and personal or large scale and systemic hurts the masses of people within the respective countries/continents. In rich countries this corruption is used to both enrich individuals as well as entrench or rescue the power of corporations whilst keeping the general populous locked in a cycle of debt slavery. In poor countries corruption kills, as the functionality of the economy is undermined and the poorest are denied the basic necessities of life.

THE ROLE OF NATIONAL CULTURE IN THE ORGANISATION OF PRODUCTION

In considering how Afrikan people have come to be so generally impoverished, we have, in a previous chapter, examined the role of individual attitudes and beliefs which are so widespread that we can say that they are to a large degree reflective of group psychology. Many Afrikan writers have written about what they call the 'Afrikan Personality' which is a term used to suggest that even whilst recognising the natural variations between individuals and between ethnic cultures within Afrika, there is a way of viewing the world, of interacting with other people and the environment which is uniquely Afrikan. Now, I would suggest that not all Black people are Black and not all Black people are Afrikan, which is to say that many biological Afrikans are psychologically Europeans or Arabs; or mentally aligned to whichever group has conquered their nation or to which they have pledged allegiance. This is how we get the nations of 'Francophone Afrika' fighting for the role of French in world affairs whilst denigrating and relegating the status of Afrikan languages to little more than the language of 'uneducated' and 'unsophisticated' peasants.

So, we have the tremendously difficult dilemma of trying to simultaneously work to recover those ideas, beliefs and values that are indigenous to Afrikan culture, whilst examining those same ideas, beliefs and values for those things that are workable and beneficial to our present situation and context and discarding those things that are not. And still we have to deal with the reality of how we actually operate today; whilst on top of all this learning from and taking the best from other cultures, whilst avoiding the danger of wholesale imitation and even further cultural colonisation!!

In other words we have a lot of work to do.

In considering the role of national or group culture, Chinweizu, in his powerful book, 'Decolonising the African Mind' makes reference to the development of what he terms *Cargo Cult Consumerism*. He tells us that Cargo Cults "arose in Melanesia in the days of European colonial rule. The Cargo Cults believed that the gods and their spirit agents were packing manufactured goods into crates, labelling them with Melanesian names and addresses, and loading them into the holds of ships and planes.......To induce these spirit agents to bring the cargo, cult members had to perform rituals involving military parades, flag raising and lowering, and meticulous observation of the rules of club organisation. And in preparation for the expected cargo, airstrips, wharves, and immense warehouses were built. Thereafter cult members would wait, and wait, and wait. Eventually the failure of the cargo to arrive would be blamed on the malice of Europeans who, it was held, had intercepted the shipments, altered the addresses, and diverted the cargo elsewhere.

These Cargo Cults arose among those peoples who had a magico-religious world outlook, who had marginal contact with industrial civilisation, who saw how the few European colonisers in their midst obtained manufactured goods, but who were unable to see, let alone understand, the nature of the manufacturing of and commerce which created and brought these goods to their shores. Fixing upon some aspects of the behaviour of the Europeans, they interpreted them as rituals for obtaining material goods from the gods. By re-enacting them, they fully expected to be rewarded, just like the Europeans." (Chinweizu 1987: 15-16)

Chinweizu goes on to suggest that the whilst the elites of the poor World may not see any connection between their policies and the aforementioned Cargo Cults, the reality is that "what have so far passed for development efforts in the Third World bear much resemblance to Cargo Cult ritualism." (Chinweizu 1987: 16) What Chinweizu was suggesting over twenty years ago was that the efforts at 'development' undertaken by governments of poor countries were based upon similarly misguided and unfounded, but firmly held beliefs about how economic development and growth are stimulated and a "superficial understanding of industrial culture." (Chinweizu 1987: 18)

In other words he is suggesting that the non-material areas of social values and modes of organisation are more important than simply building infrastructure with loans from the IMF or World

Bank and thinking that wide roads and tall buildings (built by some other people no doubt) will create an industrialised economy. I have sometimes heard Afrikans from the continent and from the Diaspora boasting about the tall buildings cluttering the skyline of this or that Afrikan city as if this were some sort of refutation of racist insults. My often unspoken question was always, who built them, for what purpose and at what cost?

Chinweizu identifies "attitudes and organizational modes which were conducive to the new type of culture and society. The processes and their results, whether capitalist or socialist, share some fundamental characteristics:

1. An acceptance of the nation state as the paramount focus of the loyalties of citizens,...
2. An ideological commitment to the desirability of national wealth and power,...
3. An ethos in which scarcity is treated as an inspiration to creativity and productivity, and not as an excuse for fatalistic sloth, prayer, idle hope and national beggardom.
4. A devotion to vigorous productivity...
5. A high value on efficiency that is harnessed to productivity through the cultivation of a work and performance ethic.
6. A constant nurturing of the habit of saving and productive investment, together with the elimination of customs and social expectations which hinder it.
7. The cultivation of a rationalist world outlook and a problem solving approach to life.
8. An industrial mode of organising production and distribution with appropriate family ad social structures to support and benefit from industrial organisation.
9. A system of effective state institutions to provide guidance, support, and arbitration services to economic organisations."

(Chinweizu 1987: 20)

In both the case of the USA and USSR which he uses as case studies there was a heavy price to pay for rapid industrialisation. In the case of the US, there was a bloody civil war, looting by robber barons such as Rockerfeller, political suppression and the virtual destruction of effective trade union organisation. In the Soviet Union there was revolution and civil war, political suppression and mass executions, Stalin's gulags, and a death toll that ran into many millions. As Chinweizu states "Whenever the costs are reckoned, it becomes clear that the fruits of industrial development did not come cheap." (Chinweizu 1987: 21)

Kwame Agyei Akoto & Akua Nson Akoto in their powerful book 'The Sankofa Movement' clearly articulate the increasing acceptance amongst a diverse range of analysts of the importance of culture in determining racial/ethnic success in an increasingly competitive world.

"There is a general consensus that the world order is indeed changing and changing rapidly. What seems to be increasingly clear is that the nation-state is diminishing in relative importance. The construct that is likely to supplant both ideology and the nation-state as the principle agent in the affairs of the world is culture. Culture is indeed reemerging as the determinant factor in human history, not class, ideology, or great men and women. Civilisation as employed by Huntington is no more than a more generalized elaboration of national culture. There is no more substantive definition of civilisation than ordered social existence. The concept of civilisation corresponds in large measure with culture, race, ethnicity and nationality. They are each expressions of essentially five factors. Those factors are:

1. Common historical background, the most substantive being three or more millennia in duration
2. Phenotypic affinity, indicating a shared genetic pool of phylogenetic proximity and linkage
3. Common psychological construct
4. Shared geographical origins

5. Shared cultural/cosmological formations and spiritual sensitivities

It is clear that culture will be the foundation of the new regional and world political and economic entities. Kotkin's conception of global tribes and Huntington's conceptualization of clashing civilisations echo a theme enunciated by Garvey eighty five years ago and confirmed with John Henrik Clarke's final mandate to the Afrikan world." (Akoto & Akoto 2000: 70)

Afrika needs to change and that change needs to be systemic, drastic and profound. Economically, Afrika is in a far more parlous state than either the Soviet Union or USA were when they embarked upon industrialising their economies. Also, we need to avoid falling into the trap of believing that we should copy what 'worked' for others in the past; since, as has been highlighted change always comes at some cost. Afrikan countries will have to find ways of providing the basics of food, clothing, shelter and security for their people. The pivotal one of these basics is security since without security and with the types of civil wars that have plagued so many Afrikan countries there is no secure basis for production. Contrary to what many people seem to believe; poor people tend to starve either because they cannot afford to buy food or because of disruption to food production or forced migration caused by military conflict. Starvation due to lack of food in a country is relatively rare. The normal response to drought is for people to migrate to where the economic going is better, however if migration routes are closed off due to military conflict people end up in huge feeding stations where disease abounds and the weak perish.

Sustainable development is a phrase often quoted as pundits debate the effects of global warming. What is clear is that development that involves consuming ever larger quantities of the world's finite resources will, in the long or short run, become unsustainable. Solar energy offers a solution to erratic domestic electrical supplies in Africa; however who is going to pay to install hundreds of millions of solar panels. Take a look in your home and see what is made by an Afrikan individual or company? Virtually nothing with electrical or mechanical parts I would wager. Therefore if you can't pay for solar panels or if your cash strapped government can't pay for them, and if your country does not have the productive infrastructure you will suffer from electricity shortages – if you can afford to pay for it in the first place.

Food production in Afrika needs to reconsidered. Fertile land is used to grow roses in Kenya for European markets which requires a huge amount of water. The roses bring in foreign currency which is needed to service the huge debts many Afrikan countries labour under. Because so much land is consumed growing cash crops food needs to be imported, costing more foreign currency and often giving locals the taste for highly subsidised foreign produce, such as US rice, leading to the decimation of local farming and food production – which has had subsidies removed by order of the IMF - and so on and so on.

The most valuable resource a people have at their disposal are their minds. Culture determines group values and helps to shape people's attitudes and behaviour in conjunction with the variances caused by upbringing and individual personality. As a people who have been conquered, Afrikans have become locked into negative, regressive, group retarding behaviours. With the reality that many Afrikans do not hold a strong allegiance to their 'race' whilst excusing the consistent record of race based attacks on Black people by Europeans and Arabs, it is no wonder that we end up having to eat sh*t sandwiches without the bread!

It is going to take brave, bold and visionary leadership to lead Afrikan countries and Afrikan people across the world, out of this mire of poverty. Black Nationalists need to fix their attention in a far more vigorous and focused way on economic development and as Baba Amefika Geuka of the National Coalition of Black Leadership suggests, become Practical Nationalists as opposed to simply Cultural Nationalists, who like most Afrikans are stuck in a mode of having to ask for what they want and beg for what they need.

Section III

The Road to Victory

INDIVIDUAL & COMMUNITY SOLUTIONS

Some Financial Do's and Don'ts to Get in the Black and stay out of the Red

- **Do** Create a household budget.
- **Do** concentrate on debt reduction. It is easier to save money than to make it.

If you are in arrears with payments do the following:

- Don't ignore the problem
- **Do contact the organisation you owe money to.** Let them know you are having problems.
- **Do get free help and advice.** E.g. Go to the Citizens Advice Bureau or equivalent outside of the UK
- **Do pay priority debts first** – for example, mortgage, rent, council tax, or gas or electricity arrears. Credit card debts are not priority debts (in the UK) although credit card companies will harass and threaten you.
- **Do think carefully before borrowing money to repay debts.** Get advice before borrowing against your home – you will pay more in the long run and risk losing your home.
- **You may be able to ask a court for more time to repay a debt** – but only in some circumstances. **Do** Speak to a debt adviser before considering court action.

- **Do** go shopping with a list
- **Do** stop and count to 20 before making a spontaneous purchase
- Even if you have a job **Do** develop additional/multiple sources of income. Look to develop this income around something you are interested in.
- **Do** read, books, magazines, websites etc. that teach you

about money management and financial literacy e.g. *www.moneysavingexpert.com*

- **Don't** take out debt to buy depreciating assets such as cars
- If interest rates are falling or low and you can afford it, **Do** 'overpay' on your monthly mortgage payments to reduce its time span
- **Do** give to a good cause(s), even if it is only a little
- **Do** spend as much as possible with Afrikan owned businesses (find out about the *local multiplier effect* and you will see why this is important)
- **Do** use price comparison sites to get the best deal on gas and electricity, mortgage rates, insurance etc.
- **Do** save regularly
- **Don't** invest more than you can afford to lose
- **Do** spread your risk by investing across High, Medium and Low risk investments
- As you get older **Do** reduce your proportion of high risk investments
- **Do** participate in some form of collective community based investment e.g. pardner, credit unions, *www.abdf.co.uk*
- If you create new income streams outside of a job, **Do** think about setting up a company to reduce the tax liabilities on your new earnings
- If you are short of cash **Do** see if you can barter services with other people

Reducing Motoring Expenses

- **Keep your tyres fully inflated.** Fully inflated tyres are more fuel efficient than underinflated tyres.
- **Replace tyres when they get worn.** Balding tyres are not only dangerous they also reduce fuel efficiency
- **Reduce your use of your car air conditioning** (if you have

air con). Use of the air conditioning increases fuel consumption.

- **Stick to the speed limit.** Driving at 80mph uses 25% more fuel than driving at 70mph.
- **Change gear at the appropriate speed.** Driving in the wrong gear increases fuel consumption.
- **Keep on the move.** Stopping and starting again uses more petrol than maintaining steady movement.
- **Too much booty** – Get rid of unnecessary loads in the boot of your car to lighten the load.
- **Keep you tank well filled.** You lose more petrol through evaporation in a fuel tank that is nearly empty.
- **Join a car club** – book a pay as you go car when you need it rather than paying the £2,000 a year costs of owning a vehicle.
- **Walk, cycle or bus it** when you have the time.

Looking after your Savings

With interest rates falling you might want to look at alternatives to a standard bank savings account.

- **Fixed rate bonds.** Even if interest rates fall further you will get a fixed rate of return with these types of bonds. You often need to invest at least £1,000+ to open a bond.
- **Consider an ISA (Individual Savings Account [UK]).** ISAs provide a tax free home for your savings.
- **Don't touch it.** You can often get better rates of return if you opt for savings accounts with notice periods or fixed-rate fixed-term accounts.

Investment Strategies

- Don't assume that diversifying your investments automatically means lowering risk. You still need to look at each individual investment carefully.

- Remember in terms of the average income:average price ratio property prices are still historically high. However there is value to be had during the current turmoil.
- Government bonds often offer a calm port in choppy waters. Gilt prices rise as interest rates fall.
- Keep some cash for a very rainy day. Keep some cash in an instant access account. You can still get some reasonable rates if you look around.
- It is often about time and not timing. If you have investments that have fallen e.g. property and you can afford to hang onto them, then the likelihood is that in time they will recover their value.
- Shop around regularly for the best savings products.
- Shop online for energy. The cheapest energy tariffs are available online.
- Don't follow the herd. By the time most people pick up on a trend the best profits have often been taken.
- Create an investment plan and maintain financial control.
- Focus on reducing your mortgage. If you can make overpayments then do.

CREATING ECONOMIC EMPOWERMENT FOR AFRIKAN PEOPLE

Introduction

This chapter is designed to highlight some key issues in transforming the economic position of Afrikan people in the UK, however many of the ideas are directly translatable to the situation of Afrikans in different countries around the world.

It was inspired by the response I received to an email I had sent out in March 2008 which was entitled 'A Day in Harlesden'. The framework was my attempt to provide a concrete workable framework to help solve the problems I had highlighted in my email (which is reproduced below) and also to stay true to the maxim - which I believe is everyone's responsibility and especially writers - if you raise a problem, then propose a solution.

Greetings

I thought I would share some thoughts on my day in Harlesden, North West London on Saturday.

I was in Harlesden to attend the London/South East regional meeting of ABDF Ltd (www.abdf.co.uk) and it proved to be highly ironic as we sat in the back room of one of the relatively few Afrikan owned businesses in that area. There we were discussing economic co-operation and development whilst outside along Craven Park Road and Harlesden High Street Afrikans were busily relieving themselves of large amounts of their hard earned money.

If you take a walk down your average High Street/Main Street/Boulevard, in any area with a reasonable Afrikan population and if your mind as well as your eyes are wide open you cannot help but notice the peculiar relationship that Afrikans, be they in Banjul, Kingston, Los Angeles, Soweto, London or anywhere else across the planet, seem to have with other racial groups. This relationship centres on the transfer of wealth, via money, from the Afrikans to the other groups. There are rituals associated with this process, such as questions, animated conversation, sometimes smiles and even handshakes; however the end result is always the same, money moves out of Afrikan pockets, wallets/purses and hands into non-Afrikan hands, wallets/purses and pockets. No wonder the Korean Grocers Association in the US emphasised to their members that they should smile more when serving Afrikan customers, as we like to receive a smile when giving our money away to other groups.

There were some interesting aspects to this transfer of wealth that I noticed on Saturday which included:

- *The Afrikan businesses that did operate in the area were almost wholly confined to selling items that can be classified as 'discretionary expenditure' such as music CDs, trainers/sneakers. The Afrikan owned food shops were all selling cooked food i.e. take away/sit down outlets rather than greengrocers selling raw produce. People will cut back on take aways before basic food items.*
- *All of the grocers outlets were owned by Indians or Pakistanis and were packed with predominantly Afrikan customers.*
- *One or two of the Asian shops allowed Afrikan street vendors to set up small stalls outside their stores selling music CDs and pumping reggae music. This gave the superficial impression of economic partnership between Afrikan and Asian.*
- *One or two of the Asian shops employed Afrikans in low level positions (lifting and toting produce), but in only one did I see an Afrikan in a position where they might be handling money!*
- *I have never seen so many Hair product shops in such a small area. These shops were not only immaculate in their signage and decor but some were very large. The mind*

boggles at how many wigs some sisters can go through and how much money is passing out of the Harlesden Afrikan community via these shops alone. It really is a sad and mind-blowing sight to see.

- *I did not see a single Asian person in the handful of Afrikan owned shops. This is no doubt due to the resistance of Asians to giving us their money and secondly the narrow range of products that most of our shops sell, many of which focus on selling almost exclusively to the Afrikan community and not to the wider community.*

The shop we were in was like a small haven or sanctuary in a sea of economic madness. The shop is the home to two businesses Miracle Textiles and Playfayre Books owned by two sisters who combined their previously two premises to work together out of the same location, thus saving money on rent, rates, utilities etc.

Perhaps living in Nottingham where there is only a small Afrikan 'community' one has higher (if unrealistic) expectations with regard to the economic development of places such as London, just as perhaps Afrikans in the UK have unrealistic expectations of Afrikans in the US with their much larger population and several majority Afrikan cities. Are these expectations unrealistic, or do they reflect the normal expectations of most people of their fellow group members, whilst our collective behaviour is symptomatic of profound psycho-cultural dysfunction? I tend to adopt the latter view and my Saturday in Harlesden has only strengthened my determination to make the ABDF a force for transformational change in the UK and eventually across the world.

We have different and real opportunities opening up to us all the while. www.livinginblack.ning.com *is one such opportunity. A chance to use technology to link up the 'conscious' community worldwide, and just as importantly at a national, regional and local level where much of the practical work needs to take place. Keidi Obi Awadu has set a target of 10,000 members by the summer. Let's spread the word and make this a reality. The big question is what will we do with this 10,000 people when we get there. Will we use it to develop concrete plans that we turn into real co-operation and businesses or just as a talking/moaning shop where we can decry the 'White Man'?*

Another opportunity is presented by the www.bringbackblack.com *campaign. A real determined effort to reignite the spirit of the 1960's to address the issues of today. Whilst US based those of us outside of that location can offer not only moral support but also build links and develop joint initiatives as the campaign develops.*

There are many other opportunities presenting themselves, it is up to us to seize the moment. That moment is now!

If not me then who? If not you then who! If not now then when?

Hope for Peace, but Prepare for economic War

Ifayomi

The following framework is not designed to provide a comprehensive summary of various economic theories or to examine international trade policy or governmental economic policy, but rather to identify some practical steps that Afrikan individuals, groups and communities can take in the short, medium and longer-term.

For those interested in gaining a much more comprehensive understanding of our current economic predicament I would suggest reading 'Blue Print for Black Power' by Amos N. Wilson. If you can't deal with an 800 plus page book try 'Black Economics' by Jawanza Kunjufu, 'Powernomics' by Claude Anderson or 'Niggers, Negroes, Black People and Afrikans' by me (selected chapters).

Economics is about who gets how much of what. It is about the allocation and distribution of resources. Whilst economic theory can be extremely complex there are some fundamentals that we all need to understand. Therefore this paper is written by a layperson for the layperson.

Basic Areas in need of Attention

There are four areas of personal and community economics that we need to address immediately. These are:

Consumption– Spending and the use of material resources

Saving – Ring fencing money or material resources to be used for future consumption or investment purposes

Investment – Directing money, time and labour towards the creation of wealth/additional resources

Production – The creation of goods or services that people need or want and are prepared to pay for with money or via the exchange of other goods and services

The diagram below illustrates in a simplistic way the contribution that these four legs of the economic stool contribute to the achievement of Afrikan economic empowerment. Reciprocally, it suggests that it is **Culture**; and the **values, worldview and strength of group loyalty** which flow from culture; that ultimately leads to the creation of group enhancing behaviours with respect to the four components, or legs, of our economic stool.

At present our economic stool has four broken legs, hence why we constantly seem to have splinters in our batty!

If you examine the above diagram you will notice that the central Culture circle is relatively faded in terms of the overlap with the Investment and Production circles. This is to reflect and represent the current situation where the drive to consume is powerful and the habit of saving is still relatively strong (particularly amongst our elders), whereas we have a very weak investment culture and have become amongst the least independently productive people in the world.

Now, let's look in turn at each of the components and identify what we would like to see changed and how we can go about changing it. We will then go on to identify the types of organisation that we need to take up this framework in order to effect this change. Neither I nor you can guarantee that any or all of them will pick up these ideas; however we can control our own individual actions and take responsibility for turning rhetoric into action and putting our time, intellect, emotional energy and money where our rhetoric is.

Consumption		
Goals	**Change Sought**	**Tools/Methods to be employed**
Reduce expenditure per household in absolute terms	• A change in attitude towards consumption • Less brand loyalty • Increase in fnancial literacy • Increased concern over environmental protection	• Link people to debt mgt services • Run financial literacy classes • Produce educational material in CD and DVD formats • Promote Xmas spending fast • Promote bartering/LETS schemes • Environmental education, promote: reduce, reuse, recycle mentality • Increase use of solar energy • Create food co-ops • Increase use of allotments and use of gardens to grow food
Increase the proportion of expenditure with Afrikan owned businesses	• Raise awareness of the consequences of spending outside the group (Local Multiplier Effect) • Increase in 'Race First' commitment • Raise profle of Afrikan owned businesses	• Promote 'Buy Black' campaign • Link campaign to loyalty card scheme • Directory of Afrikan owned businesses in paper/CD/web based formats • Promote customer service training in Afrikan owned businesses
Reduce expenditure on depreciating assets	• Raise awareness of depreciation attached to commonly purchased goods e.g. cars, TVs etc. • Attack psychological attachment to conspicuous consumer items	• Media and street level leafleting campaign to highlight how little many brands cost to make and worker exploitation • Financial literacy classes • Adult education classes addressing identity, history and group esteem

Saving		
Goals	**Change Sought**	**Tools/Methods to be employed**
Increase levels of savings per household	• Change in attitude so that saving is viewed as necessary and praiseworthy • Re-embracing of cultural heritage of 'pardner'/Susu etc.	• Financial literacy classes • Information on how to get best return on savings • Budget mgt tools • Expand existing credit unions and create new ones

Investment		
Goals	**Change Sought**	**Tools/Methods to be employed**
To increase investment levels per household	• Raise awareness of the link between investment and wealth creation • Undermine job mentality and dependency syndrome • For parents to teach their children the importance of investing	• Financial literacy classes for adults and youth • Promote investment clubs and pardner schemes and encourage them to invest in Afrikan businesses • Create more co-operative investments in local communities that benefit local communities
To increase the level of investment in Afrikan owned enterprises and in Afrika	• Link potential investors to Afrikan businesses seeking investors • Raise awareness of the many investment opportunities in Afrika • Reduce the fear of Afrika in the Afrikan mind • Improve social, cultural, psychological and economic links between Afrikans globally	• Directory of Afrikan owned businesses • Run investment seminars with business associations • Promote ethical investment in Afrika • Promote established investment vehicles such as ABDF Ltd • Increase trade missions, youth exchanges and general contact with Afrika

Production		
Goals	**Change Sought**	**Tools/Methods to be employed**
To increase the number of Afrikan owned businesses	• Improve access to investment capital • Increased entrepreneurism • Improved co-operation amongst Afrikan businesses	• Create more investment clubs and link to businesses seeking investment • Promote sectoral and geographic clustering • Promote vertical integration in key sectors
To increase the range of goods and services produced by Afrikan owned businesses	• Improve access to large scale capital to aid diversification • Promote self-employment/business ownership as viable career options amongst young	• Promote vertical integration in key sectors • Improve consumer feedback to identify needs and opportunities • Promote sectoral and geographic clustering • Build links with conscious high net worth Afrikans
To improve the quality of goods and services produced by Afrikan businesses	• Improve customer service • Improve awareness of the need to reinvest in new equipment and improved production techniques	• Encourage our most well qualified students to go into business • Afrikan owned businesses to offer more undergraduate placements • Run Black = Excellence campaign

In order to achieve the goals set out in the above table we will need to mobilise a range of individuals, groups and organisations. I have set out below some of the types of organisations that I believe could play an important role in bringing about the change we seek. The list is not exhaustive, simply a starter for ten.

Potential Organisational Drivers

Religious/Spiritual organisations
Black Churches (those with Afrikan-centred or Pro-Black ministers)
NOI (Nation of Islam)
African Hebrew Israelites
Ausar Auset
Alkebulan Revivalist Movement
Nuwabians

Non-religious organisations
PACM (Pan-African Congress Movement)
Afrikan Credit Unions
Business Associations
ABDF Ltd
National Coalition of Black Leadership (USA)
Bring Back Black campaign (USA)
Media organisations
Local independent community organisations
Traditional women's and men's societies (Afrika)
Secret societies

I have stressed independent organisations since as the saying goes 'S/he who pays the piper calls the tune' and any serious attempt to change our situation needs to be free of those Afrikans suffering from BMEitis or People of Colourism. Since this movement will inevitably bring us into conflict with other groups who currently benefit from our present self-harming consumption patterns; we must have these activities led by those who can stand firm in the face of the inevitable multi-directional attacks.

The most important organisation that needs to be mobilised in the Afrikan community is the Afrikan family. Economics has helped to undermine the Afrikan family, particularly in 'the West'; and it can contribute significantly to the reconstruction of the family.

The Missing Element

It has often been noted that if you want to change people's behaviour you need to appeal to their emotions rather than their intellect. Most of the people reading this document will be aware of many of the issues raised and solutions suggested, but will in many cases have failed to implement most of the ideas in any significant way. Similarly, many of the so-called 'unconscious' masses are well aware of our collective economic predicament, but do little to contribute to meaningful change. So, the multi-billion pound question is, how do we stir our people's hearts? I don't believe it is sufficient to simply evoke a negative i.e. racism and what has been done to us – since many of our people seem to think that's all in the past. No, we need to conjure up an image of what victory will look like, how life will be when we return to a place of dignity in the world.

From Framework to Action Plan

What has been presented in this chapter is a framework for action and not an action plan. In order to create an action plan one would need to insert timescales, success measures, resources and most importantly responsibility into the earlier tables. This work can be done by you the reader for a single element of the framework or even the whole thing if you are feeling audacious.

Endnote

So, there it is; a framework for contextualising some of the things we need to do. This is not the whole answer, but hopefully a part of the answer. I hope readers will build on and improve the ideas contained in this chapter and use them for our people's economic empowerment.

RECOMMENDED READING

Anderson, C. (2001) *Powernomics – The National Plan to Empower Black America,* Powernomics Corporation of America: Bethesda, Maryland

Grant, P. (2003) *Niggers, Negroes, Black People and Afrikans'*, Navig8or Press: Nottingham, UK

Harris, H. (2005) *The Twelve Universal Laws of Success*, LifeSkill Institute Inc: Wilmington, North Carolina

Kunjufu, J. (1991) *Black Economics – Solutions for Community and Economic Empowerment*, African American Images: Chicago, Illinois

Peet, R. (2004) *unholy trinity – THE IMF, WORLD BANK AND WTO*, Zed Books Ltd: London

Subira, G. (1986) *Black Folks' Guide to Business Success*, Very Serious Business Enterprises: Newark, New Jersey

Wilson, A.N. (1998) *Blueprint for BLACK POWER*, AFRIKAN WORLD INFOSYSTEMS: New York

COMMUNITY SOLUTION 1 - LETS
(Local Exchange Trading System)

Almost all readers will be familiar with the concept of bartering, the direct exchange of goods or services between two parties without the use of money. As was highlighted in the earlier chapter, 'Bankers – Predators in pinstripe suits', whilst useful; bartering has its limitations as societies grow in size and the range of goods and services available grows in number and complexity. LETS schemes were created to combine the benefits of bartering, which allows you to avoid using the government's fiat currency, with the flexibility and convenience that money brings. In this chapter we will provide an overview of what a LETS is, how it works and the benefits it can bring to local communities.

The following information is taken from the website *http://www.letslinkuk.org/*

How a LETS works

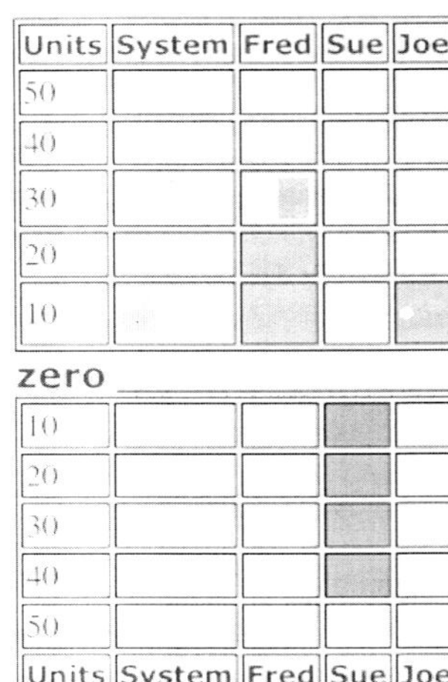

A LETS operates by Mutual Credit (i.e. currency is created by the members themselves as they transact) in a local currency equivalent to the national currency. A LETSystem is quite similar to commercial barter, but in a LETS scheme the organisers work according to a co-operative self-help model. They publish Offers & Wants listings, arrange Events, and share the administrative tasks.

The diagram illustrates the end-point of a series of transactions: Fred does a task for Sue who pays him. Joe sells vegetables to Fred who spends some of his credit. NB the hourly rate may vary. The System Account which funds administrative tasks receives an input from the members in the form of subscriptions, transaction fees or commissions so that the system is self-supporting.

NB In the LETsystem the sum of all accounts - and that includes the system account - is zero. No interest is charged for debit accounts, but a demurrage charge (for static accounts) is a theoretical option - rarely practised because it would require a more robust transaction system than most LETS have. A Community Chest may also receive regular tithing and occasional donations, to support help given to disabled members. The system account is not aware of transactions having occurred until they are recorded in member accounts.

How a Timebank works

The Timebank rewards members who do good deeds for themselves or the Community with Time Credits. Terminology is a little confusing here. The BBC Timebank issues a fiat currency expressed as hours to reward volunteering. The Timebanks UK model rewards members for engaging in community, teaching or learning activities, but also encourages "give and take" between the members: a paid "broker" responds to requests from members and matches them to those offering help.

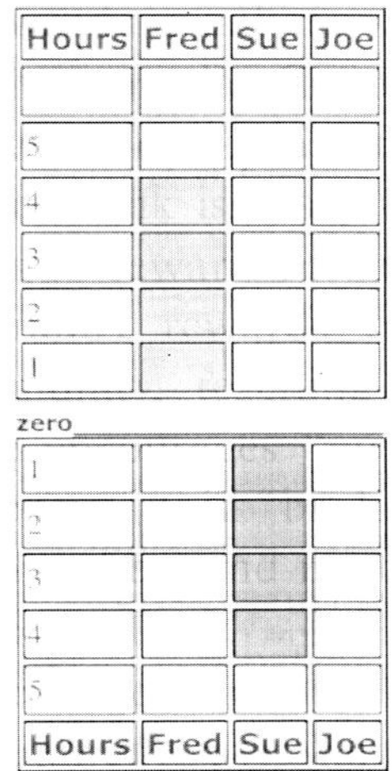

The diagram describes the same set of trades as above, in a modified way: When Sue needs help she calls the Broker who arranges for Fred to do the task and later transfers time-credits to his account from her account. In theory Joe can't sell his vegetables as there is no way of recording their value, but if the Timebanks issues "vouchers" these begin to accrue a monetary value.

No system account is needed as the administration is paid for by external funding. Time-credits are created as required but require some form of "authority" to organise and approve the activities. The activities of members are known in advance to the Timebroker, and the organisation takes care over issues of identity, police-checking, insurance, access to vulnerable members, and keeping a record of what has taken place.

VARIATIONS of the LETS Model

LETSystems take **transaction fees**, either flat-rate or commission-based, and management is non-representative. LETSchemes take regular **subscriptions** and are co-operatively run. Another option is demurrage (levying inactive accounts). LETS may have a mixture of these methods. Administration may be centralised or devolved using web-transactions. Passbooks and/or vouchers may facilitate face-to-face transactions.

SIMILARITIES between Timebanks and LETS

Many LETS members prefer to work for an equal rate of pay and many schemes are either constituted on this basis or suggest a standard rate to be used as required. Some schemes have "brokering" as one of the administrative tasks which can be devolved by type or location.

Combined Time-LETS Models

A number of LETS organisers are now working on combining LETS and Timebanks as described above. The new models range from simply working side-by-side and sharing resources to truly integrated hybrids.

LETSystem provide a good description of LETS systems in general and their variant at their website http://www.gmlets.u-net.com/faq.html

Principles and Philosophy.

What is a LETSystem?

A LETSystem is a trading network supported by its own internal currency. It is self-regulating and allows its users to manage and issue their own 'money supply' within the boundaries of the network.

The key points include:

- **co-operation:** no-one owns the network.
- **self-regulation:** the network is controlled by its users.

- **empowerment:** all network users may 'issue' the 'internal currency'.
- **money:** money, as a means of exchange, is an integral feature.

Is a LETSystem a type of barter system?

LETSystems use their own type of 'money' - they are money systems.

Barter is a type of exchange where we swap goods and services without using money - I give you a loaf of bread and you give me two cabbages. You fix my car and I'll cook you dinner. But you may not like my cooking...

Money overcomes the limitations of barter. I give you money for your goods and services and you can spend it elsewhere. In a LETSystem you can use your account to buy what you want from one person and then sell what you can to another.

What does LETS stand for?

The word "LETS" was chosen to highlight an invitation (let's) and a culture of consent. LETS embodies the 'Law of Two Feet' - "If you like it, you walk in. If you don't, then you walk away".

LETS supports trading which results in win-win outcomes. This is to be contrasted to the more coercive types of behaviour often seen in communities which are short of money - "I've got the money, so you have to work for me." In LETS, there is never any obligation to trade.

The use of LETS as an acronym was an afterthought. The most common rendering is 'Local Exchange Trading System'.

What is the basis of LETS?

LETS is based on the value of the individual within the community. This involves both freedoms and responsibilities. We can outline the main criteria:

- **consent,** nothing happens without it.
- **no interest** to be charged on account balances.
- **common ownership,** resulting in cost-of-service provision of support services.

- **disclosure of information** – to ensure the informed action of users.

How do people value goods and services within a LETSystem?

Using the pound sterling as a convenient measure, prices in the sterling economy provide a starting point. But valuations in a 'local' economy tend to differ from those outside. Activities which are traditionally low-paid tend to be rewarded more generously. On the other hand, activities which are conventionally more highly-paid tend to trade at lower prices.

This is a function of the way the LETSystem operates. The differences result from using a 'money' which is not in short supply and which is only acceptable to other users of the system. No intervention is required for this to take place, except education - and even that can be self-education.

Money does not value people, people value each other. But, when money is scarce, valuations become distorted. For example, I want to give you as little money as possible, for as much as I can get from you. By using a 'money' that is not scarce, people are able to value each other more appropriately.

What are the benefits to individuals?

Individuals can benefit through greater access to goods and services; through more affordable training and education; additional employment; starting a business - there are many possibilities. In addition there are more intangible benefits which also improve the quality of life, such as the widening of social networks.

COMMUNITY SOLUTION 2 – ABDF Ltd (Afrikan Business Development Fund) *www.abdf.co.uk*

Those of you who have read some of my previous books will be familiar with the ABDF Ltd or Afrikan Business Development Fund. To summarise briefly, it is an economic development company with a hybrid co-operative/traditional limited company method of operating which drew its original inspiration from the *Pardner* schemes which my parents' generation brought with them to England from the Caribbean. Pardner is also known as Susu in parts of West Afrika and the technical name for it is a rotating credit association. The difference between what we do in the ABDF and a traditional pardner (there are a number of variations, particularly in West Afrika) is that in the ABDF, none of those investing into the pot takes a 'draw' instead the money is left to accumulate and then invested collectively on behalf of all investors.

The ABDF is the practical antidote to all the cheap Black talk about the need for us to put our money together and invest. When I first got into this 'Black ting', as some sceptics call it, I used to be energised by this talk until I quickly discovered that many of the talkers weren't doing anything of the sort. I have given talks up and down the UK and in some countries overseas as well and I often ask three questions:

1. How many of you present have heard people talking of the importance of Afrikan people putting our money together?
2. How many of you think it is a good idea?
3. How many of you are engaged in collective investment with other Afrikans?

You know when people talk about separating out the wheat from the chaff! Normally, 100% of hands go up in response to question 1. Between 95-100% of hands go up to question 2 and about 10% of hands go up to question 3. I have previously articulated my belief that about 1% of Afrikans in the UK, US etc. are Pan-Afrikanists and of this 1% only about 10% are practical Pan Afrikanists; ready to give real substance to their words. Forget Du Bois' talented tenth; it is the practically conscious 1/1000th that have to carry the load! However thankfully it is not all doom and gloom since there are another group of Afrikans, whom I refer to as the Pro-Blacks (see my previous book 'Why Willie Lynch Must Die'), who; whilst they are not strongly ideological, do love Black people (they are not always fully comfortable with calling themselves Afrikan if they are not born in Afrika or of direct Afrikan extraction), are often more practically minded than the Pan-Afrikanists, are much larger in number and on average definitely have more disposable income than the Pan-Afrikanists.

Pan-Afrikanists, based upon my experience in the UK at least, generally tend to be more interested, skilled and knowledgeable in Health and Nutrition, Education, Metaphysics and History. They tend to be less interested and skilled in business development, management and organisational development. Luckily whilst the pro-Blacks are generally weaker in the Pan-Afrikanists' areas of strength they tend to be stronger in their areas of weakness. Put the two groups together and we have ideology, practicality, numbers and money!

The ABDF was founded on 2nd November 1996 and became a limited company in May 2001. As of May 2009 there were around 125 Afrikan women and men shareholders who had committed to investing collectively for their individual and community betterment. In addition there were another ten or so people whose applications for membership had been accepted but who had not yet commenced making payments and so were not yet shareholders.

After a long battle to persuade investors of the need to increase their level of investment there was a significant increase in average monthly investments during 2007 which coincided with the push to raise capital to finance our proposed investment in Ghana and by May 2008 the average monthly investment was around £40 per month. Notwithstanding this long overdue and welcome increase in investment levels the ABDF remains totally committed to being accessible to Afrikans of all income levels who share our vision and support our principles and the minimum monthly contribution has remained at £5 per month for the unwaged and £10 per month for the waged for several years.

Despite the extremely low cost of getting involved; the ABDF has been subject to accusations of 'elitism' from some who should know better, but obviously don't. The main reason for this criticism seems to centre around the relatively high incomes earned by some – but by no means all - ABDF members and the significant number of ABDF investors who have degrees or other higher level qualifications. The critics' argument seems to be that if you cannot exactly reproduce the socio-economic and educational profile of our national population then you are elitist. The ironic thing is that these critics are nearly always people who have higher than average income levels and/or higher than average qualification levels. I keep waiting for them to set up the perfect economic development organisation, but then of course they normally have a problem with making money and wealth creation and so prefer to rely on sporadic donations to finance their endeavours.

These people can only see that the glass is half empty and so of course only see the ABDF investors who are Lawyers, Accountants and Doctors, but not those who are Factory Workers or Lorry Drivers! Anyway, the only way to avoid making mistakes is to stay under the bedcovers for the whole of your life so I guess destructive criticism comes with the territory, just like positive and constructive criticism; which is to be welcomed.

The simple reality is that the people most likely to join something like the ABDF in its early days - and yes even after nearly 13 years I consider these to be the early days, as I will explain later on – are those people with a relative degree of *emotional space* and a level of financial room for manoeuvre. In the years and decades to come I fully expect the so-called *masses* to come on board, however the reality is that this is only likely to happen **after** we have proven ourselves a financial success story and not whilst we are proving ourselves a financial success story. Until then; we will keep on working together and growing and working and growing.

So, given all of our hard work and dedication to date why haven't huge numbers joined the ABDF? Well, I have come up with following reasons, which have either been explicitly stated or implied by people I have encountered whilst promoting the ABDF over the years:

- They don't believe in Afrikans organising for any kind of power
- They are extremely cash strapped
- They don't believe in making money and generating wealth. However they are happy with a donations culture where they take donations from people who work for the system they constantly decry
- They are financially comfortable and don't see any need to engage in group economics. These people have been conditioned to believe that success for Afrikan people is just about individuals competing – which they are good at – and not individual competition combined with group co-operation.
- People who have *privatised* their lives.
- People who were activists in the past, but who have become disillusioned.
- Hopeless procrastinators
- People who experience chronic distrust of other Afrikans
- People already engaged in collective investment

The Psychological disposition of investors in the ABDF during the course of its development

One can assign psychological dispositions to the investors who join ABDF at various stages of its development

The Pioneers – These are the trailblazers, the people who set up the organisation in the face of naysayers, critics and overcoming self-doubt. This also includes those people who developed ABDF in towns/cities/regions where we formerly did not have a presence and those people who will set up the first branches of the ABDF or its equivalent overseas.

The Early Joiners – These are those people who were just waiting to find something they could believe in and join. These people are positive and optimistic by nature.

The Practicalists – These people are hard headed and will judge an initiative based upon its demonstrable merits. If a business can demonstrate competence of leadership and a strong vision they will be prepared to get involved.

The Wagonists – These are the largest group of people. Followers of fads, fashions and trends. They will get on board when the case is made and the going is good. No sentiment, little race loyalty – initially at least – just show me the money/emotional gratification/status/balm for my wounded soul etc.!

As mentioned earlier, in my opinion the ABDF is still in its early stages of growth and its development can be compared to the development of a human being over their lifetime. If one were to take the notional period of 80 years as an average life expectancy (in the rich world) one can divide this organisational life cycle into four stages: Developmental, Global Expansion, Consolidation and Transformation. These stages are analogous to the four stages of the human life as described by Herbert Harris in his book 'The Twelve Universal Laws of Success' (2005). The life stages as described by Harris are: Education, Sensation and Experience, Power and Legacy.

So let's review the ABDF's past.

Developmental Phase 1996-2016 0-20 (Childhood and Adolescence)

0-13 ABDF Childhood (1996-2009 [The Past to Present])

You may well be familiar with the story of how the ABDF was conceived and gestated in the eight months prior to its birth on 2nd November 1996. I wrote the original proposal for the creation of the ABDF on two sides of A4 paper folded in half; and had in the back of my mind the development of an organisation that would do more than simply financially advantage its members – although that remains one of our primary goals. The vision, which at the time I did not feel confident enough to articulate, was to create an organisation of truly transformative size and power. Twelve plus years on, as ABDF Ltd comes to the end of its organisational childhood it is now the right time for us to set out a vision for the organisation's long term future.

The first thirteen years, like human childhood, have been a time of relatively slow growth and enormous learning. We have put together the organisational structure or skeleton upon which we are now able to develop the fleshy muscle which is represented by the membership.

As this text was being written the company was completing a review of its structures, processes and procedures to make it fit for purpose for the challenges ahead. Those challenges include:

Short term challenges

- Distance managing the investment in our Ghanaian company
- Developing the administrative capacity to manage mass membership
- Creating organisational capacity to handle 'internationalisation'
- Delivering profits and paying dividends
- Dealing with the issue of Interest and equitable finance

Long term challenges

- Maintaining the ethos whilst devolving power
- Raising the consciousness of the membership
- Grooming the new generation of leadership and achieving leadership transition
- Developing a vibrant youth wing
- Delivering transformational change in Afrika whilst delivering sufficient profits and dividends to keep investors on board

- Managing disruption from agents of the Caucasian power structure

The only things that are certain are that it is going to be an exciting ride and that failure is not an option!

There is Another Way – Ending the Economics of Brutality

This chapter provides an overview of the book 'The Real Wealth of Nations' (2007) by Riane Eisler. In this book she analyses the cultural origins and social, economic and environmental impact of what she terms 'the economics of domination'. The central thesis running throughout the book is that domination systems of economics results from a deeply entrenched patriarchal order that diminishes and demeans all form of social or economic activity that is viewed as feminine or female – hence the low status accorded to caring activity - whilst valorising competition over co-operation and any activity that is viewed as masculine or 'men's work'. As Eisler notes "people think nothing of paying plumbers, the people to whom we entrust our pipes, $50 to $60 per hour. But child care workers, the people to whom we entrust our children, are paid an average $10 an hour.....And we demand that plumbers have some training, but not that all child care workers have training." (Eisler 2007: 16)

She also notes that "The U.S. company Salary.com estimated that a fair wage for a typical stay-at-home parent would be $134,471 a year." (Eisler 2007: 19)

In order to create a fairer more Caring Economic System Eisler suggests there are six fundamental foundations that must be put in place and these are:

Foundation 1: A Full Spectrum Economic Map

Foundation 2: Cultural Beliefs and Institutions That Value Caring and Caregiving

Foundation 3: Caring Economic Rules, Policies, and Practices

Foundation 4: Inclusive and Accurate Economic Indicators

Foundation 5: Partnership Economic and Social Structures:

Foundation 6: An Evolving Economic Theory of Partnerism

Source: *Eisler 2007: 22-23*

In terms of creating a full spectrum economic map Eisler highlights how traditionally a large portion of activity that is essential to the maintenance of society has been completely excluded from the definition and measurement of economics and economic activity. She describes what she describes as 'the old economic map' in the diagram below:

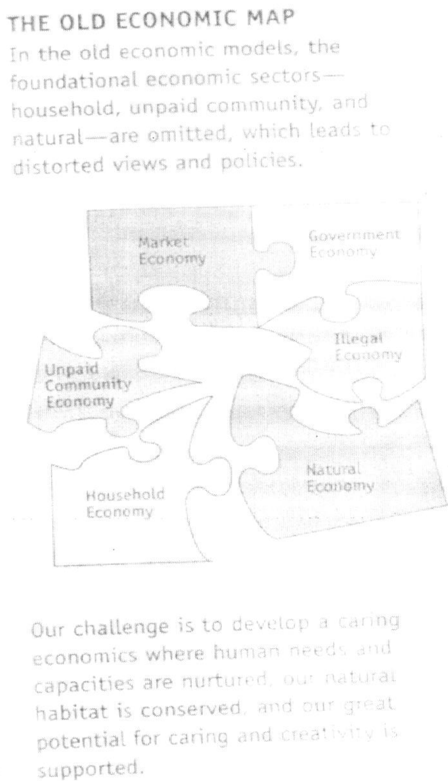

Source *Eisler 2007: 13*

Whilst setting out the 'new economic map' as in the diagram below:

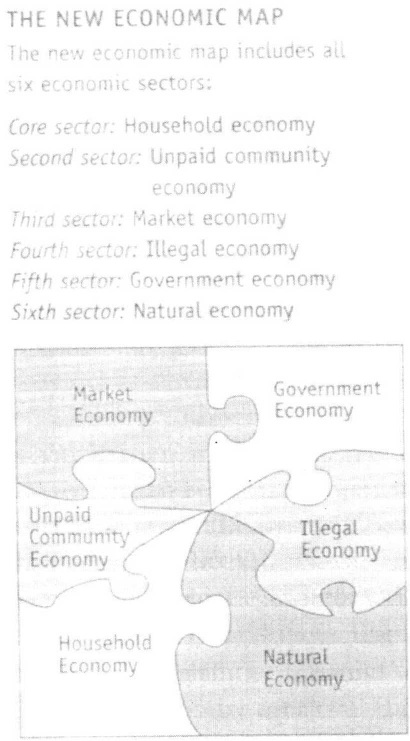

Source *Eisler 2007: 12*

In reflecting upon how 'women's work' is normally omitted from measures of economic production Eisler notes that "The 1995 United Nations Development Report estimated that the value of women's unpaid work is a whopping $11 trillion per year, and noted that "if national statistics fully reflect the 'invisible' contribution of women, it will become impossible for policymakers to ignore them in national decisions. ... If women's unpaid work were properly valued, it is quite possible that women would emerge in most societies as the major breadwinners – or at least equal breadwinners – since they put in longer hours of work than men."" (Eisler 2007: 84-85)

Eisler in describing capitalism and socialism suggests that "both are still caught up in the dominator "conquest of nature" and have given little value to environmental housekeeping." (Eisler 2007: 32) She also notes how both work according to the old economic map and how the founding intellectual fathers of both systems, be it Adam Smith or Karl Marx, pay scant attention to the economic role of women, caring and the household economy.

Eisler also notes how economic scarcity can be artificially created (in capitalism to create profit). She notes that one definition of economics that remains popular is "the social science that studies the allocation of scarce resources to satisfy unlimited wants." (Eisler 2007: 33)

However she notes that "Although scarcity is caused by natural conditions, as we will see, dominator economic systems artificially create and perpetuate scarcity – and with this, pain and fear. They do this through misdistribution of resources to those on top, heavy investment in armaments, lack of investment in meeting human needs, ruthless exploitation of nature, and waste of natural and human resources from wars and other forms of violence – all of which are inherent in the domination systems. (Eisler 2007: 33)

She describes what she sees as "Dominator Economic Assumptions

- The main motivations for work are fear of pain and scarcity.
- People cannot be trusted.
- "Soft" qualities and activities are inappropriate for social and economic governance.
- Caring and caregiving are impediments to productivity, or at best irrelevant to economics.
- Selfishness will lead to the greater good of all."

Eisler 2007: 34

The aforementioned cultural expression of dominator economic assumptions perhaps find their ultimate expression, amongst the leading economies of the world, in the USA. This *'dog eat dog'* economic Darwinism leads to the concentration of wealth in the hands of a small proportion of the population as set out below:

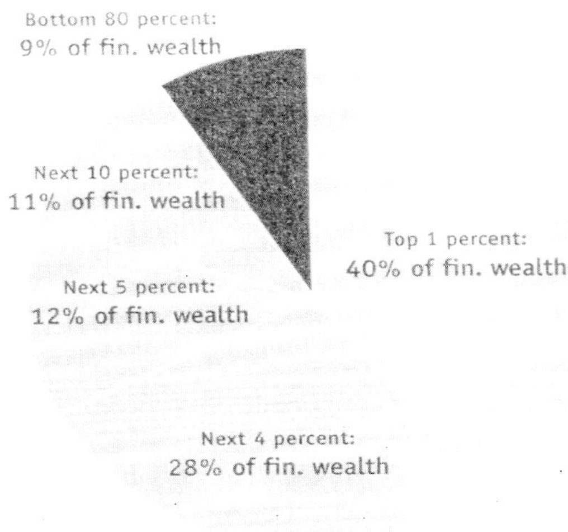

FINANCIAL WEALTH DISTRIBUTION, 2001[23]

In relation to the above diagram Eisler cites G. William Domhoff who says "Since financial wealth is what counts as far as the control of income–producing assets, we can say that just 10 percent of the people own the United States of America." (Domhoff cited in Eisler 2007: 41)

In describing the critical dynamics of the partnership and domination systems Eisler suggests that:

"There are two basic human motivations. One is avoiding pain. The other is seeking pleasure. These motivations operate in both the partnership and domination systems, but the motivation is different in each.

In the domination system, fear of pain is a major motivation. This can be fear of punishment from "superiors" or fear of losing power and status. Consequently, much of earlier thinking about effective workplaces was based on the belief that the more employees feel threatened, the harder they will work.

Today, most business experts recognize that people actually

perform better when they are not afraid, when they feel safe and cared for rather than threatened and unsafe.” (Eisler 2007: 105)

The diagram below provides a pictorial representation of these two approaches.

DYNAMICS OF THE PARTNERSHIP/DOMINATION CONTINUUM

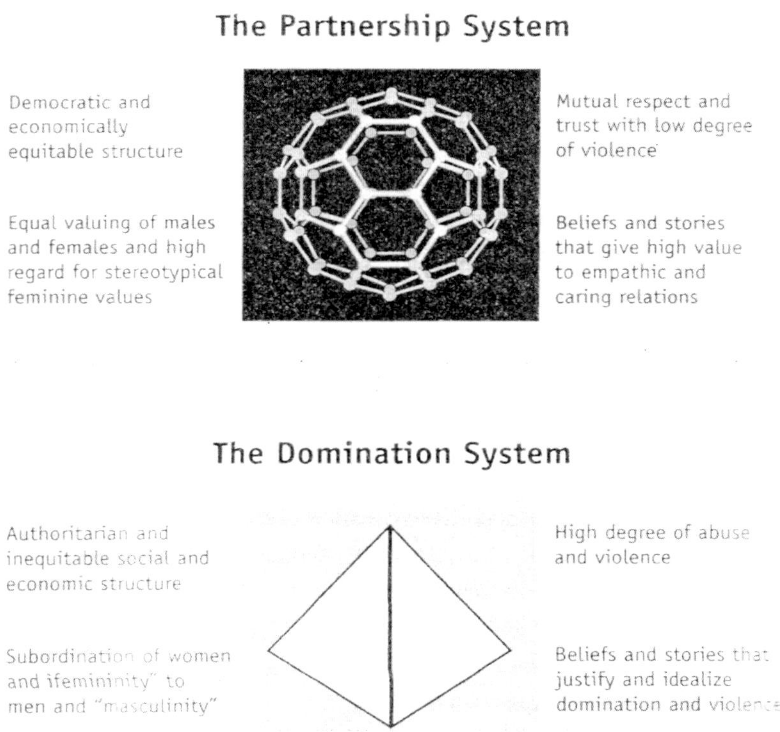

The relationship among the components of each of these two systems is interactive, with all four core components reinforcing one another. These interactions shape all social institutions and relations, including economic ones.

Source: *Eisler 2007: 104*

Eisler clarifies that “partnership social and economic structures still have hierarchies. However....these are..hierarchies of actualization rather than hierarchies of domination.” Eisler 2007: 113

A Way Forward Without Wall Street

In terms of understanding what the Wall Street financial elite are trying to achieve with the latest global financial crisis which they have engineered, Stephen Lendman in an article entitled 'Obama's War On Labor' suggests their goals are to:

- "crush world economies;
- recapitalize the IMF to entrap developing economies in perpetual debt bondage, neo-feudalism, a virtual dystopia;
- structurally adjust their populations to a living hell - impoverishment through "shock therapy" loss of employment, essential benefits, and democratic freedoms;
- tank financial markets;
- destroy competitors;
- use trillions of taxpayer dollars to consolidate the FIRE sector (finance, insurance and real estate);
- buy other assets on the cheap;
- buy toxic ones from each other, mostly with public money paying the cost and assuming the risk;
- declare war on labor; and
- force companies to downsize, then strip workers of their rights and futures.

Social Security, Medicare, and Medicaid are next to supply more funds for Wall Street, selected corporate favorites, and generous amounts for military adventurism, global imperialism, and a homeland police state apparatus to quell restive opposition when it erupts. Obama's promised change is betrayal of the constituency that elected him. Looking ahead, things appear very grim." (Lendman 07 April 2009)

David Korton (2009) makes a compelling case for the elimination as opposed to reform of Wall Street. He suggests that,

"Efforts to fix Wall Street miss an important point. It can't be fixed. It is corrupt beyond repair and we cannot afford it. Moreover, because the essential functions it does perform are served better in less costly ways, we do not need it. Wall Street's only business purpose is to enrich its own major players, a bunch of buccaneers and privateers who find it more profitable to expropriate the wealth of others than to find honest jobs producing goods and services beneficial to their communities. They walk away with their fees, commissions, and bonus packages and leave it to others to pick up the costs of federal bailouts, gyrating economic cycles, collapsing environmental systems, broken families, shattered communities, and the export of jobs along with the manufacturing, technology and research capacities that go along with them." (Korton: 45 2009)

Riane Eisler suggests some foundational steps that need to be taken to move towards what she describes as a 'caring economics'. These measures include:

1. "Recognize how the cultural devaluation of caring and caregiving has negatively affected economic theories, policies, and practices.
2. Support the shift from dominator to partnership cultural values and economic and social structures.
3. Change economic indicators to give value to caring and caregiving.
4. Create economic inventions that support and reward caring and caregiving.
5. Expand the economic vocabulary to include caring, teach caring economics in business and economics schools, and conduct gender specific economic research.
6. Educate children and adults about the importance of caring and caregiving.
7. Show government and business leaders the benefits of policies that support caring and caregiving, and work for their adoption." (Eisler 2007: 43)

Eisler provides numerous examples of how investing in caring makes not only moral sense but also good business sense. E.g. "Companies rated by *Fortune* as the best places to work also yielded shareholder returns on investment of 27.5 percent, much higher than the Russell 3000 stocks, which only had average returns of 17.3 percent." (Eisler 2007: 51)

Eisler emphasises that implementing caring policies is not just for large businesses but can work for small businesses. She cites the work of Ben Cohen and Mal Warwick who suggest that small businesses with a caring approach focus upon five basic relationships as depicted in the diagram below.

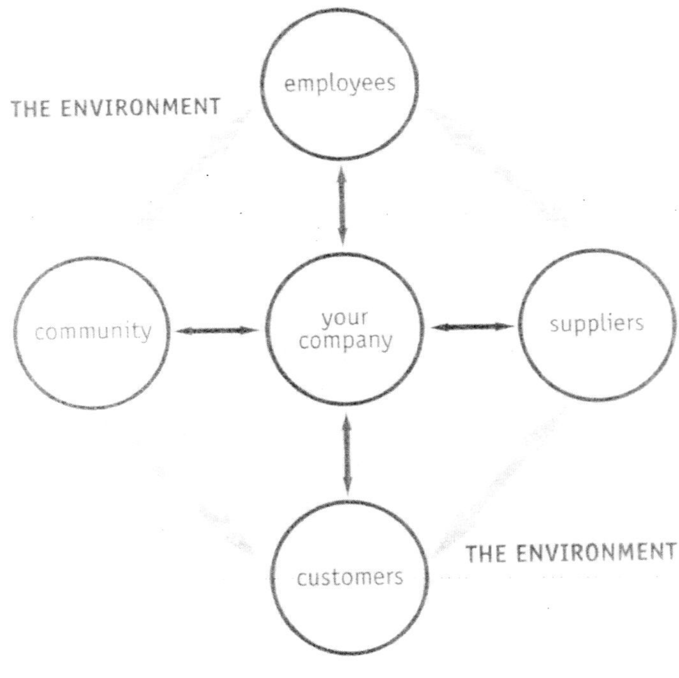

THE FIVE DIMENSIONS OF VALUES-DRIVEN BUSINESS

The fifth relationship depicted is that with the environment.

In terms of how we can all make a difference Eisler suggests the following positive actions that we can all take:

1. Change the conversation about economics to include the word 'caring'.
2. Highlight examples of how companies implementing caring policies are succeeding.
3. Promote the adoption of corporate charters that promote high standards for caring policies and behaviours by chambers of commerce and business associations.
4. Buy from companies that have caring personnel, consumer and environmental policies.
5. Support political candidates who support caring economics.
6. Teach caring skills to both boys and girls

Eisler's book makes interesting and though provoking reading and if many of the ideas she proposes were implemented the world would most certainly be a better place to live.

With regard to some other steps that can be taken to fundamentally change the nature of national (and hence global) economics I would suggest the following:

- The elimination of central banks
- Governments to take control of the issuance of their national currencies
- The elimination of fractional reserve lending
- An end to the economic growth equals inevitable good paradigm in the rich world. "Beyond a minimal threshold of consumption, building community, rather than increasing the consumption of stuff, is the key to increasing human health and happiness." (Korton 37: 2009)
- A fundamental redistribution of the resources stolen by

the global elites to assist the billions living in absolute poverty

- An end to the charging of interest on money. Or if interest is to be allowed for it to be charged by companies chartered to serve the public good and where the profits from moneylending are recycled back into the public purse.
- A curtailment of limited legal liability for corporations and an end to corporate personhood.
- Ban corporate donations to politicians and political parties and curtail political lobbying
- For polluting companies to pay for the costs of their degradation of the environment e.g. oil companies in the Niger Delta
- An end to the private ownership of land beyond that used for personal residential use (with a cap on the footprint of such homes). Where individuals or companies wish to utilise additional land it should be freely available for long-term lease. All land should be viewed as common land bequeathed by the Creator for the common good to be utilised and cared for to enable future generations to likewise benefit from its fecundity and bounty.
- A reduction in the production and consumption of meat which is an inefficient use of land
- The development of a more self-sufficient localised economics with people encouraged to consume local produce where practical.
- For the majority Afrikan; Afrikan countries (sometimes referred to as 'Black African') to avoid getting locked into the dead end that is the AU (African Union), for both political, military, economic and basic survival reasons. It would be better for these countries to focus on developing the regional continental economic blocs e.g. ECOWAS and building economic links with the worldwide Afrikan population.

There is nothing natural or inevitable about the dominant economics of brutality and exploitation. What man can do (wo)man can undo.

ENDNOTE

So, this is the end of our journey across some rough economic terrain. I wanted to keep this book as short as I could in order to encourage irregular readers to pick it up, read it and use it, however the wide array of topics that had to be covered meant that this work is longer than I had first anticipated. To reach the non-readers (by choice or through literacy problems) amongst our people I will be producing a DVD to reinforce the messages contained in this book. In addition in February 2009 I launched a community based economics and financial literacy course 'Black Economics for Human Development' which was piloted in Bristol, London and Bradford. My hope is that this course will cement the ideas detailed in this book and stimulate real change in local communities.

Afrikan people are (generally) currently stuck in the behaviour, psychology and material circumstances of a conquered, oppressed, victimised and victim minded people. The wheel of group fortune turns too slowly for most of us. We are desperate to see the transformation of our people's lives within our lifetime. However most people simply cry, moan, pray, shout and bleat for change, without acting to bring it about.

Be the change you want to see in the world and since there is no time like the present; get to work.

BECAUSE FREEDOM ISN'T FREE!

BIBLIOGRAPHY

Akoto, K. & Akoto, A. (2000) THE SANKOFA MOVEMENT – REAFRIKANISATION AND THE REALITY OF WAR, Washington DC: Oyoko InfoCom Inc

Ani, M. (1996) YURUGU: AN AFRICAN-CENTERED CULTURAL CRITIQUE OF EUROPEAN CULTURAL THOUGHT AND BEHAVIOR, Trenton, NJ: Africa World Press

Carruthers, J.H. (1999) Intellectual Warfare, Chicago: Third World Press

Chandler, W. (1999) 'Ancient Future – The Teachings and Prophetic Wisdom of the Seven Hermetic Laws of Ancient Egypt'

Cheatwood, T-H (1995) 'To Save the Blood of Black Babies – The D.C. and New York Dialogues' Richmond, Virginia: Native Sun Publishers

Chinweizu, C. (1987) Decolonising The African Mind, Lagos, Nigeria: Pero Press

Chinweizu, C. (2007) Black Enslavement: Arab and European Compared Black Power Pan Africanism (BPPA) TRACT #2 (Unpublished)

Chinweizu, C. (2007) COMPARATIVE DIGESTS 1] Racism: Arab and European compared

Chomsky, N. (1996) World Orders Old and New, New York: Columbia University

Eisler, R. (2007) THE REAL WEALTH OF NATIONS – CREATING A CARING ECONOMICS, San Francisco, USA: Berrett-Koehler Publishers Inc.

Grant, P. (2005) Blue Skies for Afrikans – Life and Death Choices for Afrikan Liberation, Nottingham, United Kingdom: Navig8or Press

Harford, T. (2007) THE UNDERCOVER ECONOMIST, London: Abacus

Harris, H. (2005) 'The Twelve Universal Laws of Success', Wilmington, NC: LifeSkill Institute Inc

Kwaw (2006) The Whirlwind newspaper, Issue 3, London: Alkebulan Revivalist Movement

New Internationalist Magazine March 2004, Vol. 10, Issue 11

New Internationalist Magazine October 2008, Issue 416

Pollard, E. (1995) Oxford Paperback Dictionary, Oxford: Oxford University Press

Peet, R. (2004) Unholy Trinity – THE IMF, WORLD BANK AND WTO, London: Zed Books

Petras, J. (2007) Rulers and Ruled in the US Empire – Bankers, Zionists, Militants, Atlanta, Georgia: Clarity Press, Inc.

Rodney, W. (1981) How Europe Underdeveloped Africa, Washington DC: Howard University Press

Subira, G. (1986) Black Folks Guide to Business Success, Newark, New Jersey: Very Serious Business Enterprises

T'Shaka, O. (2005) THE INTEGRATION TRAP: THE GENERATION GAP, Oakland, California: Pan African Publishers and Distributors

Vallely, P. (2005) Independent Newspaper, 09 September 2005, Independent News & Media (UK) Ltd.

Ward, B. & Lewis, J. (2002) Plugging The Leaks – Making the most of every pound that enters your local economy, London: The New Economics Foundation

Website references

'Additional Thoughts on the Bailout', Paul Craig Roberts, October 16, 2008 www.Information Clearinghouse.com

'A Futile Bailout As Darkness Falls On America' Paul Craig Roberts www.Information Clearinghouse.com

http://www.countercurrents.org/roberts190209.htm Paul Craig Roberts - 'President of Special Interests' 19 February 2009

www.Countercurrents.org Stephen Lendman - 'Hunger Plagues Haiti and the World', 29 February 2008,

http://www.countercurrents.org/lendman070409.htm 'Obama's War On Labor' By Stephen Lendman 07 April, 2009

www.Countercurrents.org Dmitry Orlov – 'The Five Stages of Economic Collapse', 13 November 2008

http://www.countercurrents.org/lendman151208.htm Stephen Lendman - 'Excess Debt And Deflation = Depression' 15 December 2008

http://www.countercurrents.org/lendman270309.htm Stephen Lendman - Obama's Latest No Banker Left Behind Scheme 27 March, 2009

http://www.countercurrents.org/lendman190409.htm Stephen Lendman - 'Barack Obama: Crime Boss' 19 April 2009

http://www.ft.com/cms/s/0/a4cbe81e-de84-11dd-9464-000077b07658.html?nclick_check=1 website accessed 15 January 2009

http://www.globalresearch.ca/index.php?context=viewArticle&code=HUD20090317&articleId=12328 Finance Capitalism Hits a Wall The Oligarchs' Escape Plan – at the Treasury's Expense by Prof. Michael Hudson 17 February 2009

http://www.globalresearch.ca/index.php?context=va&aid=12784 The Real AIG Conspiracy by Prof. Michael Hudson 18 March 2009

http://www.gmlets.u-net.com/faq.html

www.houseofknowledge.org.uk

http://www.independent.co.uk/news/uk/this-britain/battle-of-edmonton-chaos-as-6000-rush-for-bargains-at-ikea-opening-482859.html

http://www.investopedia.com/terms/u/utilities_sector.asp

http://beginnersinvest.about.com/cs/bondbasics/f/whatisabond.htm

http://www.investopedia.com/terms/f/financial_sector.asp

http://www.investopedia.com/terms/c/consumer_cyclicals.asp

http://www.investopedia.com/terms/b/basic_materials.asp?viewed=1

http://www.investopedia.com/terms/e/energy_sector.asp

http://www.investopedia.com/terms/c/consumerstaples.asp

http://ipsnews.net/news.asp?idnews=45335 website accessed 11 January 2009

http://www.letslinkuk.org/

http://www.lewrockwell.com/higgs/higgs102.html accessed on January 6, 2009

Licensed Kleptocracy for Years to Come The ABCs of Paulson's Bailout By Michael Hudson October 21, 2008 "Counterpunch" http://www.informationclearinghouse.info/article21066.htm

Cynthia McKinney: Ruminations on President Obama's Tenure Thus Far and "Acceptable Punditry" March 02, 2009

www.moneyasdebt.net 'Money as Debt' by Paul Grignon and produced by Moonfire Studio (a Lifeboat News Video Production)

www.nowandfutures.com/forecast.html

www.pbs.org/wgbh/aia/part1/1h295b.html

http://reactor-core.org/america-created-money.html

http://therealnews.com/web/index.php?thisdataswitch=0&thisid=1358&thisview=item

www.timesonline.co.uk article by David Charter from the Times Newspaper online on 21 February 2008

http://wakeupfromyourslumber.blogspot.com/2006/01/money-101.html (posted Friday 13 January 2006)

www.webofdebt.com Brown, Ellen - 'It's The Derivatives, Stupid! Why Fannie, Freddie, AIG Had To Be Bailed Out' (posted 20 September, 2008)

http://en.wikipedia.org/wiki/Capital_goods

www.zeitgeistfilms.com

ABOUT THE AUTHOR

Ifayomi Grant was born in Edmonton, North London, in 1966, the second of three children. He was schooled in Edmonton and Enfield until the age of 18. He has worked in a variety of roles in the Midlands, including running his own recruitment consultancy business, working in prisons and with ex-offenders as an Employment/Training Adviser, working as a Training & Development Manager, Community Safety Consultant and in his final job as the Deputy Chief Executive of a multi-million pound neighbourhood regeneration programme where he had overall responsibility for project delivery, partnership working and Human Resource issues. In February 2006; Ifayomi completed the circle and returned to self-employment and he now works as a writer as well as operating his own consultancy firm.

Ifayomi is an active member of the Afrikan community in Nottingham and is involved in a number of community groups, most notably: Nubian Link *www.nubianlink.org.uk* a community education group, ABDF Ltd *www.abdf.co.uk* (formerly Afrikan Business Development Fund) a community economic development company which he conceived and co-founded, Vice-Chair and co-founder of the Nottingham Black Families in Education Parent Support Group *www.nbfe.co.uk* which provides educational advocacy and support. In 1998 he helped found Brother II Brother; an Afrikan men's group delivering rites of passage programmes which came to the end of its lifecycle in May 2008. He also helped to create the Empower Group, a support group for Afrikans working in mentoring, which over time has transformed to become a group of friends who support each other on their life journeys.

Ifayomi is the son of Orinthea and Reuben Grant. He is married to a beautiful Afrikan queen Beverley and they have two lovely children Jawanza Kwesi and Abiba Ashia Orinthea. He has an elder brother Nigel and a younger sister Tracey.

To contact the author please email him at: *ifayomi@ntlworld.com*

Visit his website *www.houseofknowledge.org.uk* where you can buy his books, DVDs and CDs online, subscribe to his free newsletter,

'The Navig8or', and read unpublished essays by the author.

If you would like to invite the author to speak to your group or organisation please email him at the address above.

Other Books by Ifayomi Grant

Niggers, Negroes, Black People and Afrikans
Blue Skies for Afrikans
Saving Our Sons
Sankofa the Wise Man and his Amazing Friends
Why Willie Lynch Must Die

DVDs and CDs available

Why Willie Lynch Must Die (DVD)
Why Willie Lynch Must Die (CD)
Saving Our Sons (DVD)
Saving Our Sons Part II (DVD)
Creating Blue Skies for Afrikans (CD)
Building Black Economic Power (CD)
Guns and Gangs (CD)

Coming Soon

The Colour of Money DVD – This DVD will provide audio and visual reinforcement of the messages contained in this book. Ideal for teaching young people or groups about financial literacy and community economic development. Thanks to Azaniagem Greenidge for her assistance with providing film footage. Email Ifayomi for release date.